PAPER & PENCIL
GAMES
For 2 Players

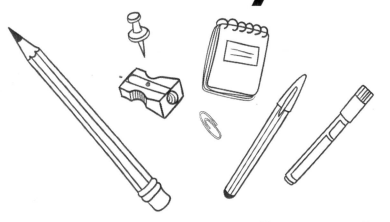

Travel Games for Kids
in Car or Plane

Here are some rules

TIC TAC TOE

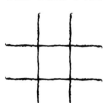

You are X and your friend is O. The first player to get 3 of hismarks in a row (up, down, across, or diagonally) wins.

3D TIC TAC TOE

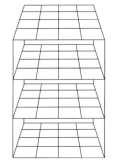

You are X and your friend is O. The first player to make a line of four cells in any direction wins.

OBSTRUCTION

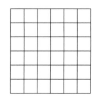

One player is 'O' and the other is 'X'. Players take turns in writing their symbol in a cell. The restriction is that you can only play in a cell if all its neighbours are empty. The first player unable to move loses.

HANGMAN

One player thinks of a word or short phrase an marks out blanks for each letter. Second player will guess a letter. If that letter is in the word(s) then write the letter in everywhere it would appear, and cross out that letter in the alphabet. If the letter isn't in the word then add a body part to the gallows (head, body, left arm, right arm, left leg, right leg).The player will continue guessing letters until he can either solve the word (or phrase) or all six body parts are on the gallows.

DOTS AND BOXES

Players take turns in drawing lines between dots on a grid. The player who completes the most boxes wins. The two players take turns to join two adjacent dots with a horizontal or vertical line. If a player completes the fourth side of a box they initial that box and must draw another line.When all the boxes have been completed the winner is the player who has initialled the most boxes.

One player is Red and second is Blue. Players alternately draw a line between two dots. The first player to draw a triangle of their color between three dots loses.

HEXAGON

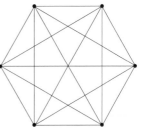

FOUR IN A ROW

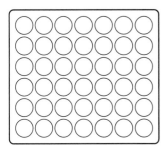

The goal of the game is to connect four of your tokens in a line. All directions (vertical, horizontal, diagonal) are allowed. Players take turns putting one of their tokens into one of the seven slots. Always add a token from the bottom of te grid!

Have a nice game!

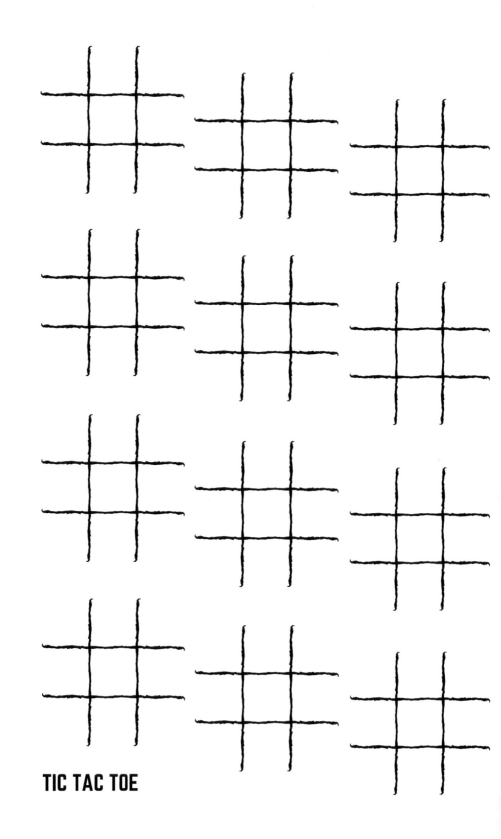

TIC TAC TOE

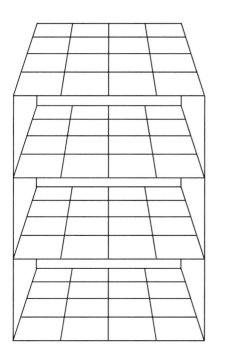

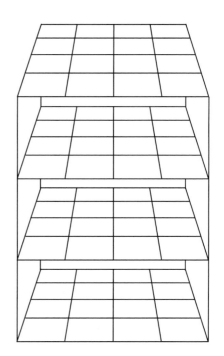

3D Tic Tac Toe

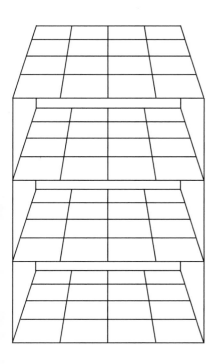

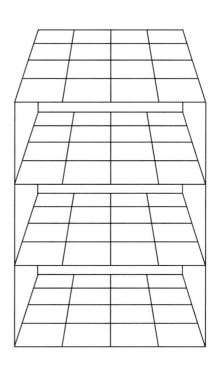

Obstruction

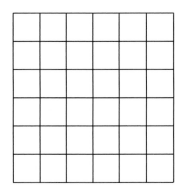

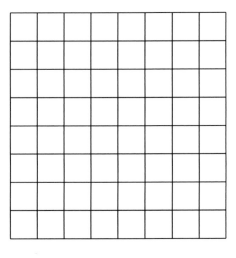

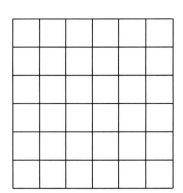

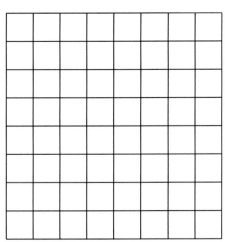

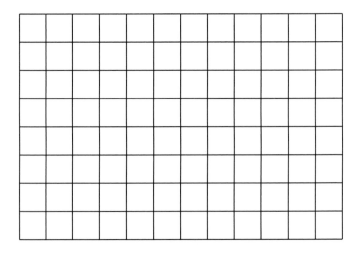

A B C D E
F G H I J
K L M N O
P Q R S T
U V W X Y
Z

_ _ _ _ _ _ _ _ _ _ _ _

_ _ _ _ _ _ _ _ _ _ _

HANGMAN

A B C D E
F G H I J
K L M N O
P Q R S T
U V W X Y
Z

_ _ _ _ _ _ _ _ _ _ _ _

_ _ _ _ _ _ _ _ _ _ _

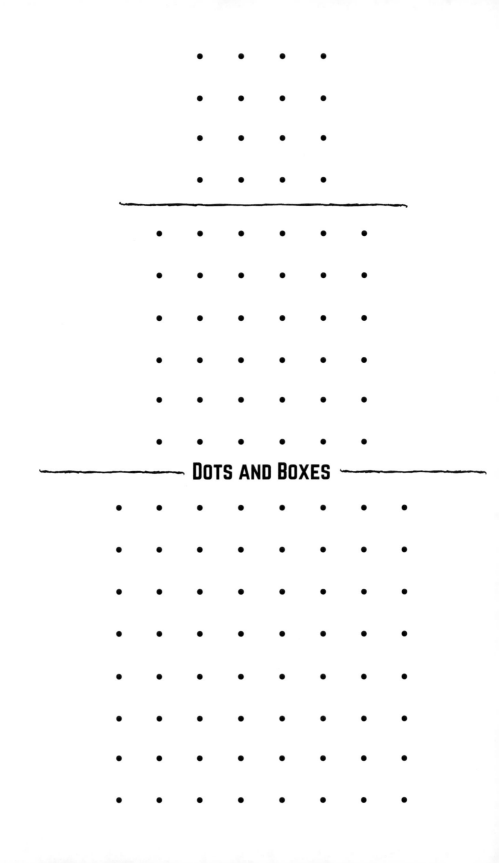

DOTS AND BOXES

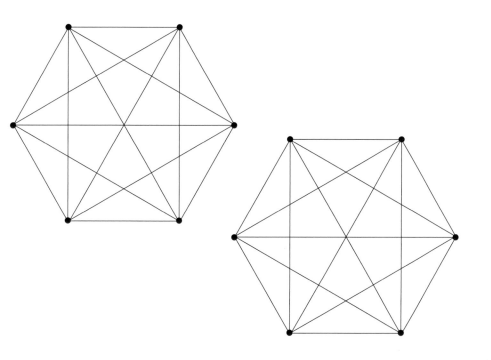

HEXAGON

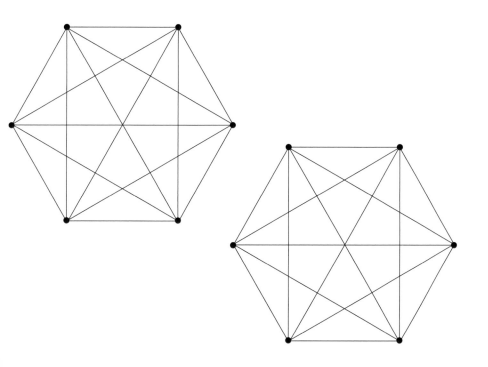

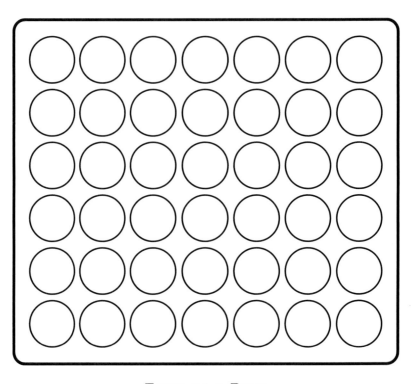

FOUR IN A ROW

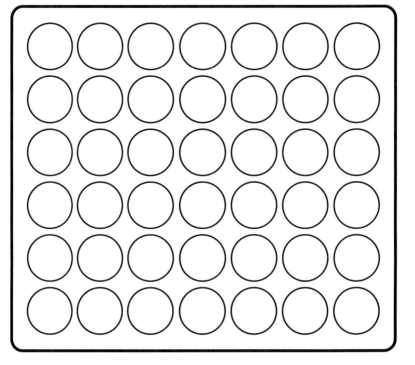

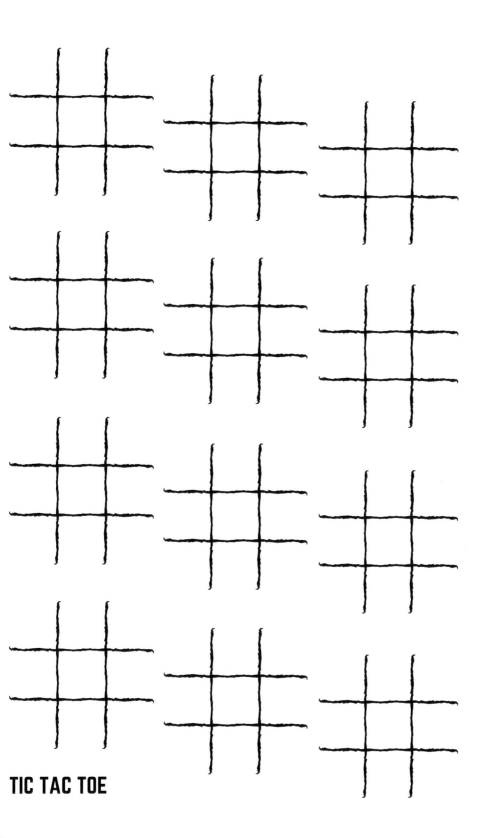

TIC TAC TOE

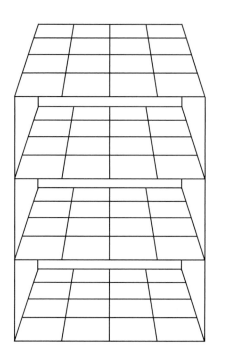

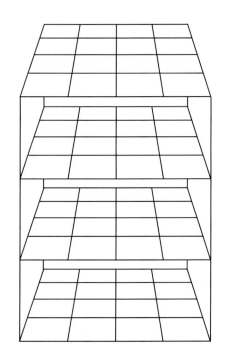

3D Tic Tac Toe

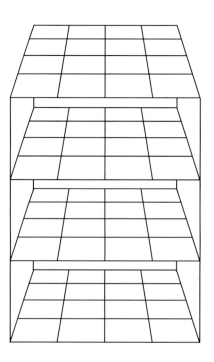

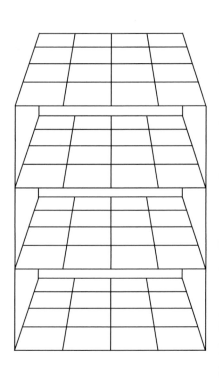

Obstruction

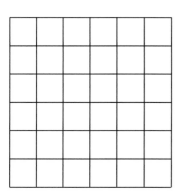

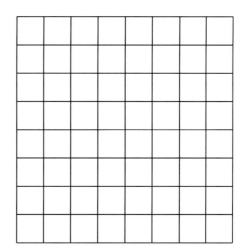

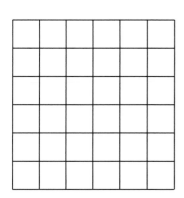

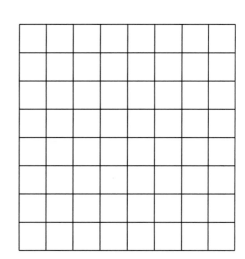

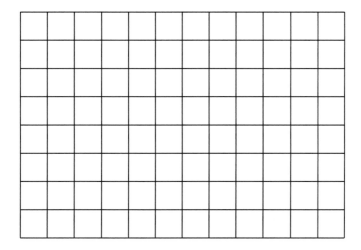

A	B	C	D	E
F	G	H	I	J
K	L	M	N	O
P	Q	R	S	T
U	V	W	X	Y
Z				

— — — — — — — — — —

— — — — — — — — — —

HANGMAN

A	B	C	D	E
F	G	H	I	J
K	L	M	N	O
P	Q	R	S	T
U	V	W	X	Y
Z				

— — — — — — — — — —

— — — — — — — — — —

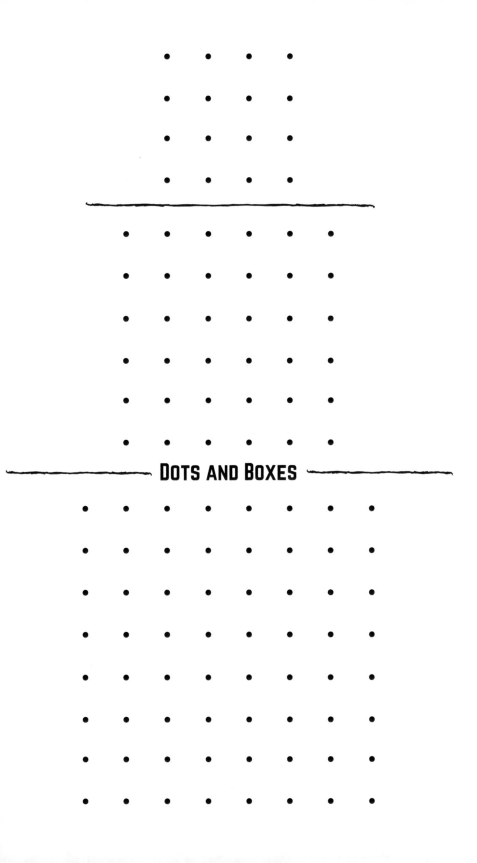

DOTS AND BOXES

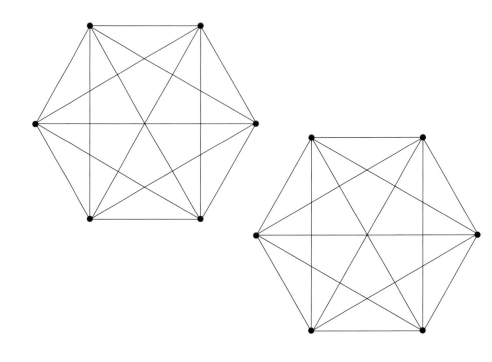

HEXAGON

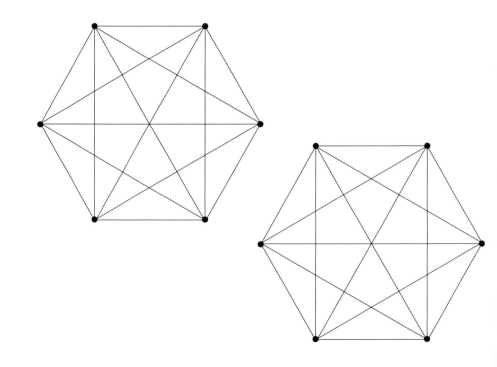

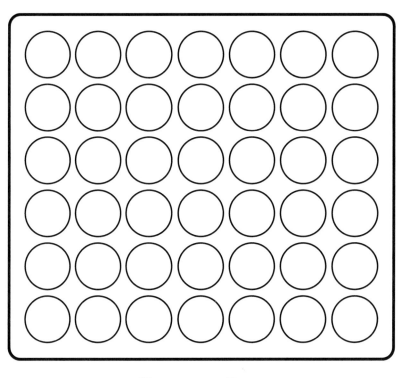

FOUR IN A ROW

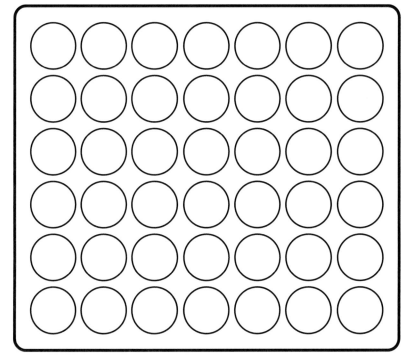

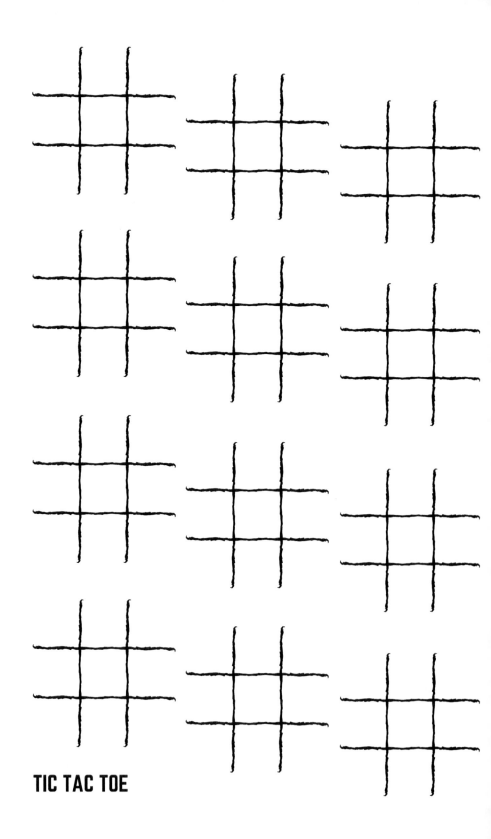

TIC TAC TOE

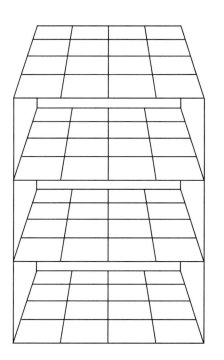

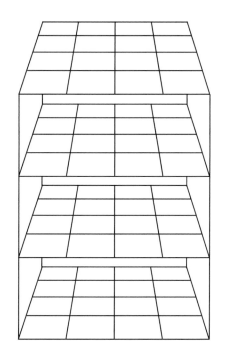

3D Tic Tac Toe

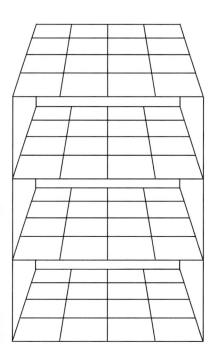

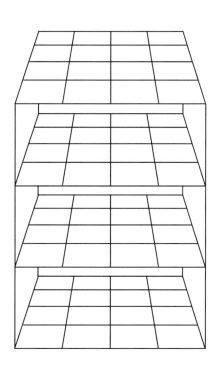

Obstruction

ABCDE
FGHIJ
KLMNO
PQRST
UVWXY
Z

_ _ _ _ _ _ _ _ _ _

_ _ _ _ _ _ _ _ _ _

HANGMAN

ABCDE
FGHIJ
KLMNO
PQRST
UVWXY
Z

_ _ _ _ _ _ _ _ _ _

_ _ _ _ _ _ _ _ _ _

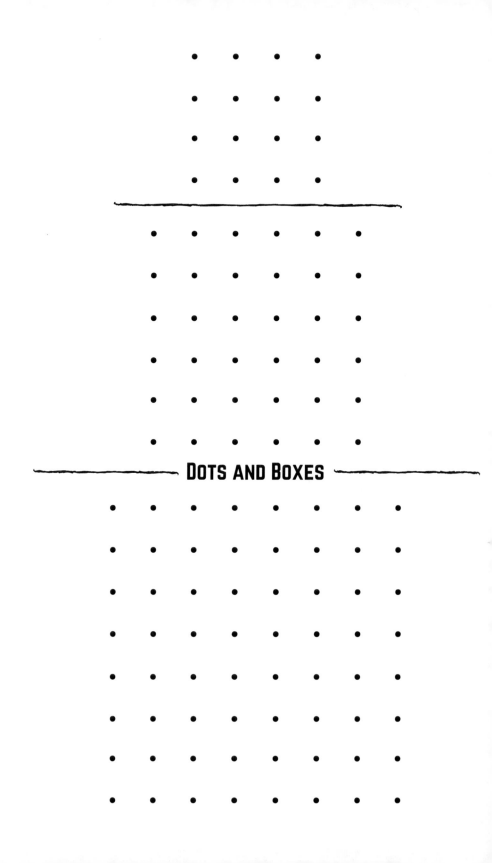

DOTS AND BOXES

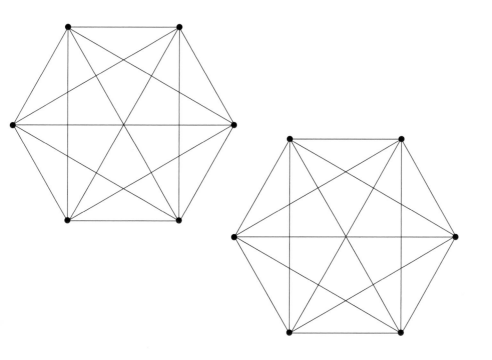

HEXAGON

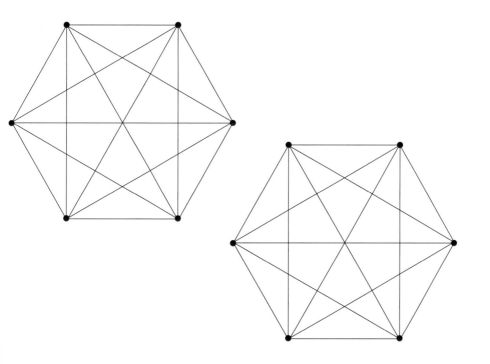

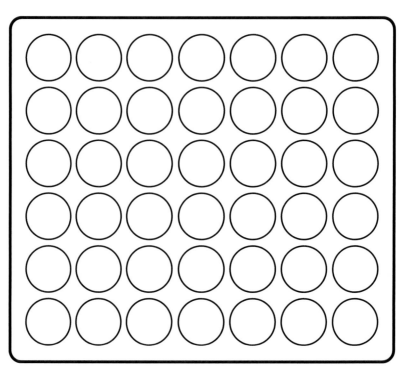

Four in a Row

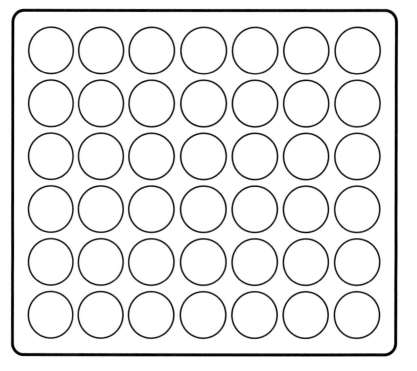

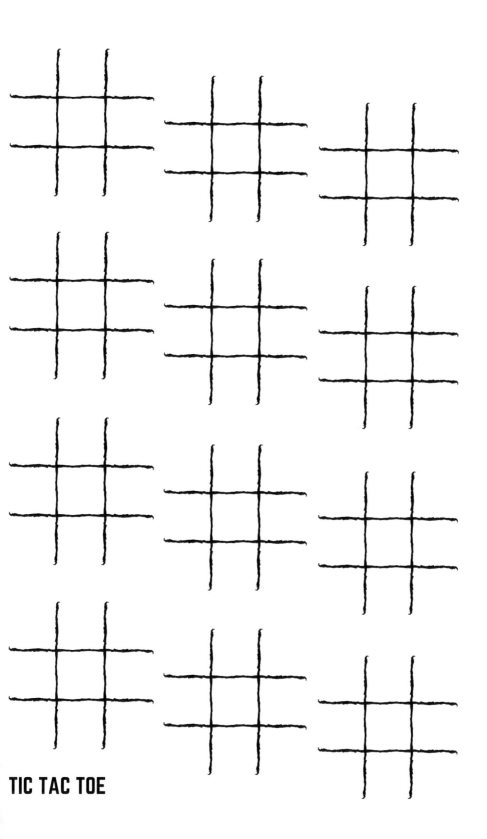

TIC TAC TOE

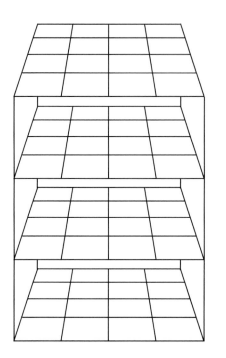
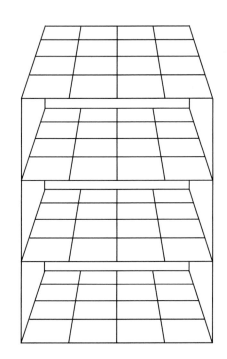

3D Tic Tac Toe

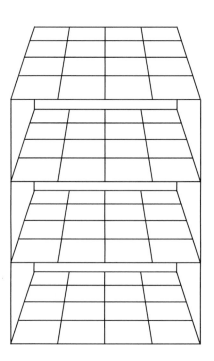
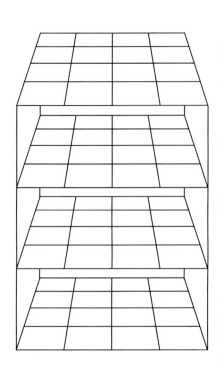

Obstruction

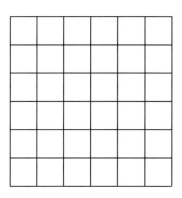

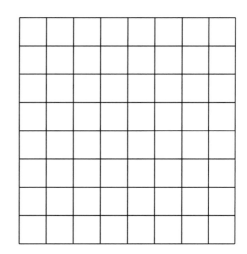

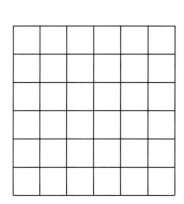

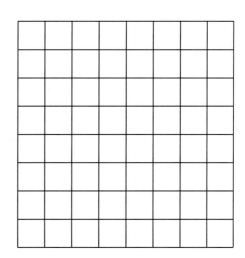

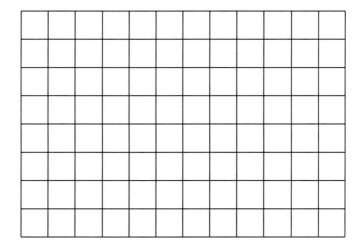

A	B	C	D	E
F	G	H	I	J
K	L	M	N	O
P	Q	R	S	T
U	V	W	X	Y
Z				

__ __ __ __ __ __ __ __ __ __ __ __

__ __ __ __ __ __ __ __ __ __ __ __

HANGMAN

A	B	C	D	E
F	G	H	I	J
K	L	M	N	O
P	Q	R	S	T
U	V	W	X	Y
Z				

__ __ __ __ __ __ __ __ __ __ __ __

__ __ __ __ __ __ __ __ __ __ __ __

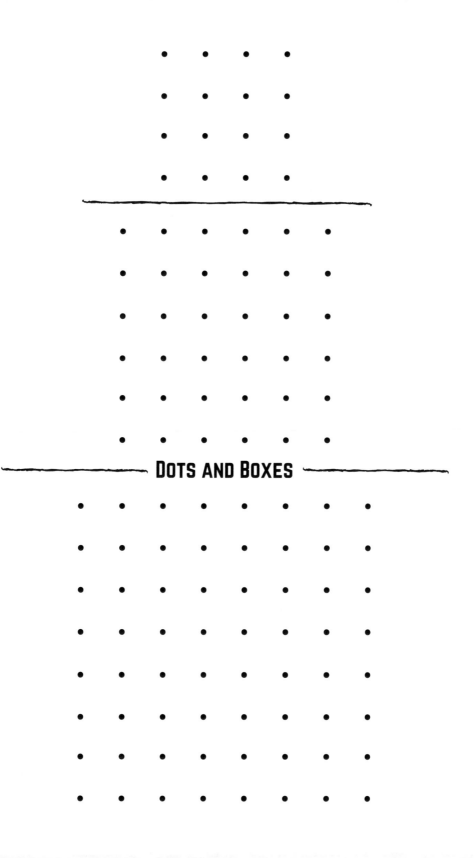

DOTS AND BOXES

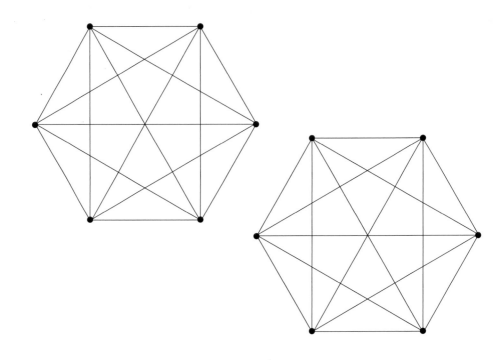

HEXAGON

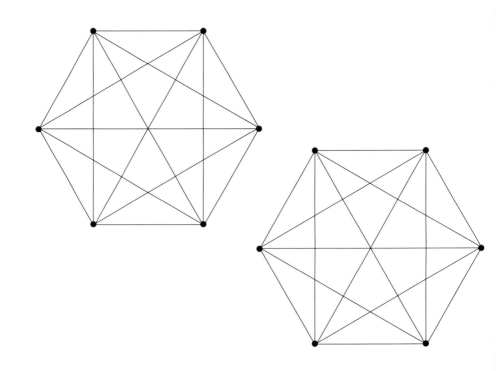

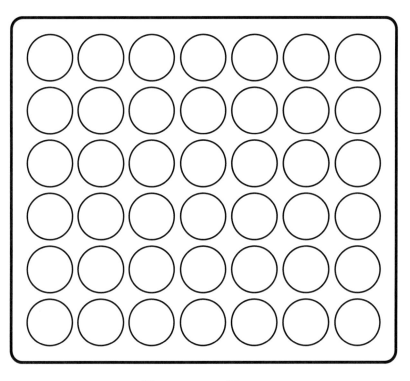

Four in a Row

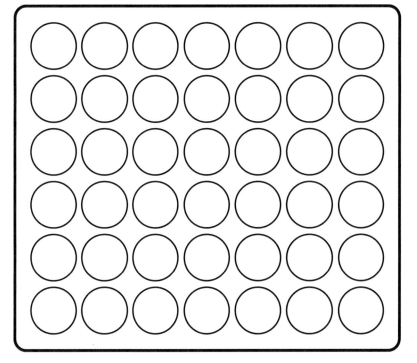

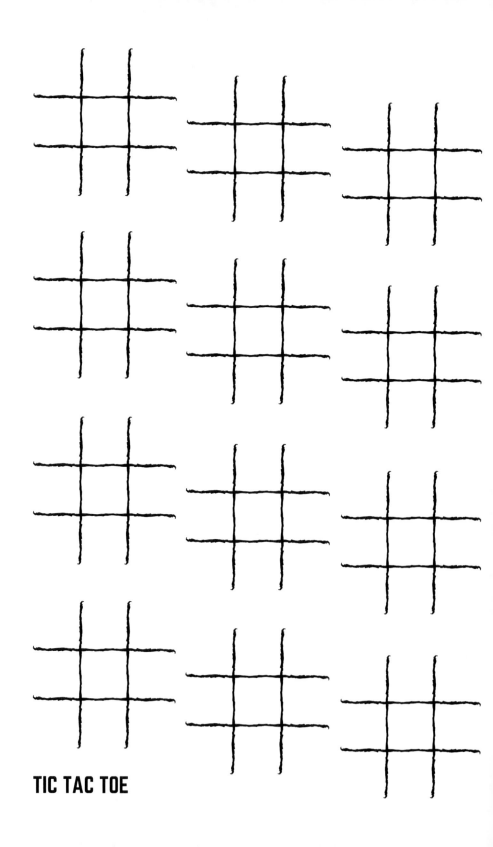

TIC TAC TOE

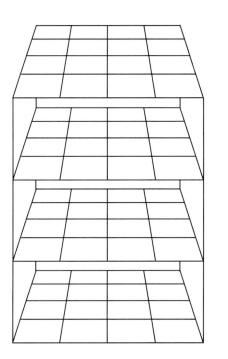

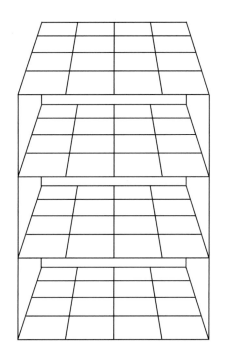

3D Tic Tac Toe

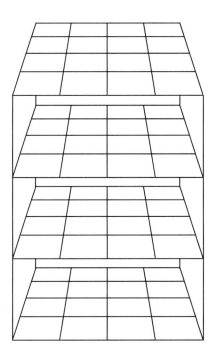

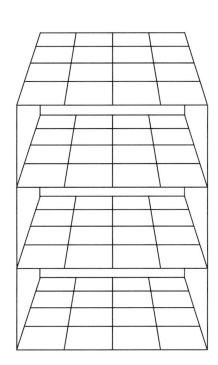

Obstruction

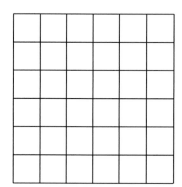
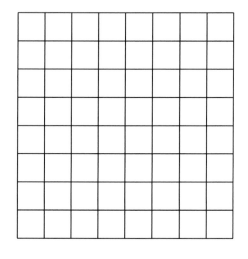
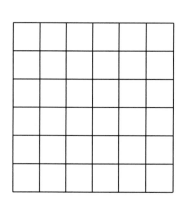
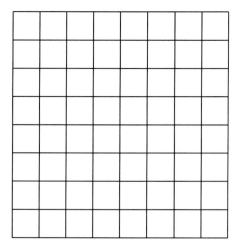
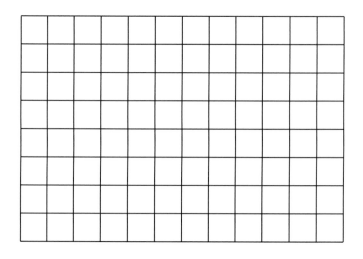

A B C D E
F G H I J
K L M N O
P Q R S T
U V W X Y
Z

_ _ _ _ _ _ _ _ _

_ _ _ _ _ _ _ _ _

A B C D E
F G H I J
K L M N O
P Q R S T
U V W X Y
Z

_ _ _ _ _ _ _ _ _

_ _ _ _ _ _ _ _ _

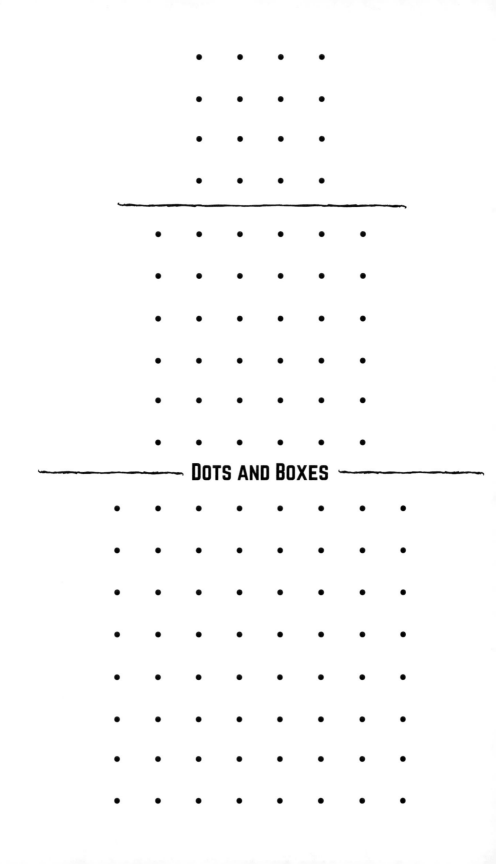

DOTS AND BOXES

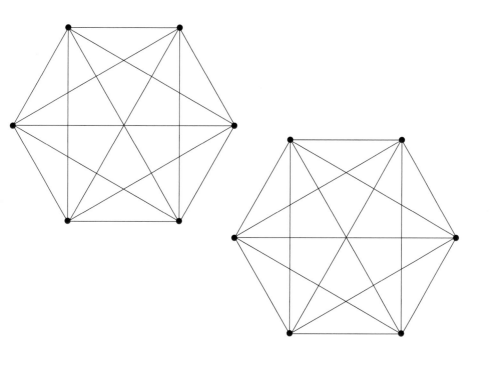

HEXAGON

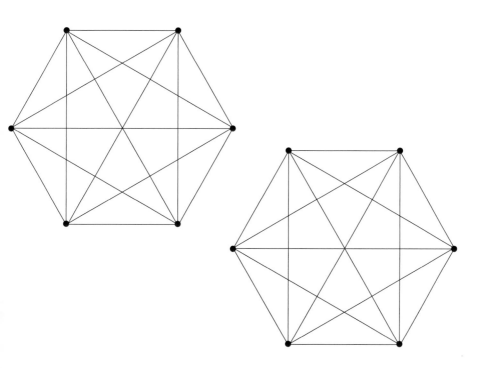

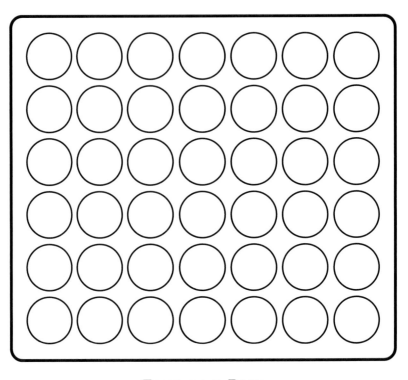

Four in a Row

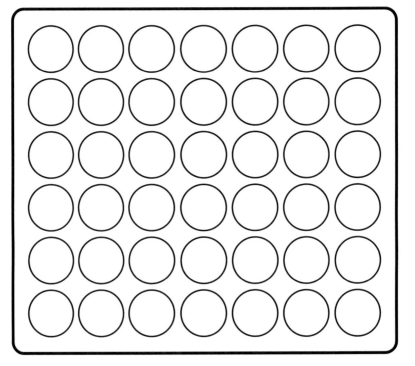

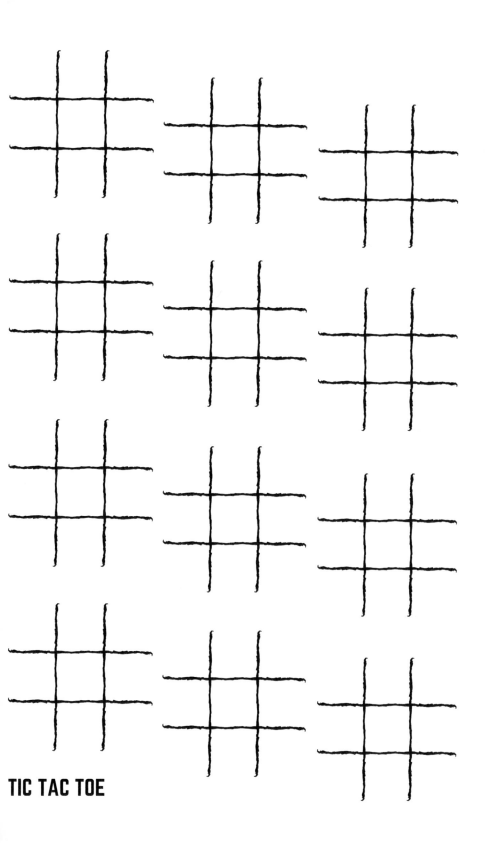

TIC TAC TOE

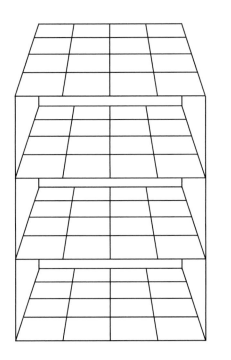
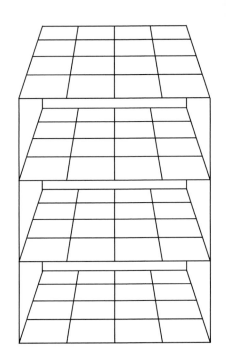

3D Tic Tac Toe

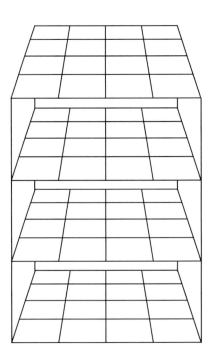
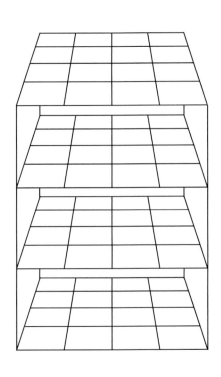

Obstruction

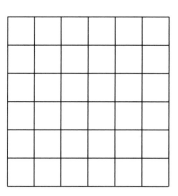

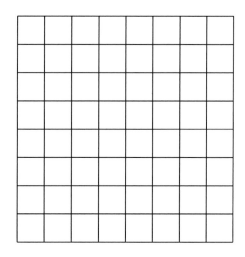

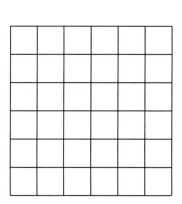

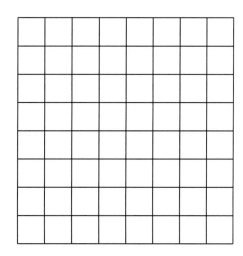

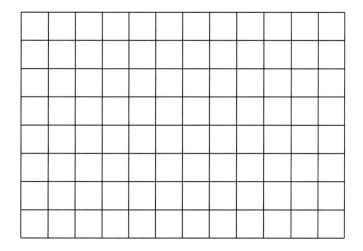

_ _ _ _ _ _ _ _ _

_ _ _ _ _ _ _ _ _

HANGMAN

_ _ _ _ _ _ _ _ _

_ _ _ _ _ _ _ _ _

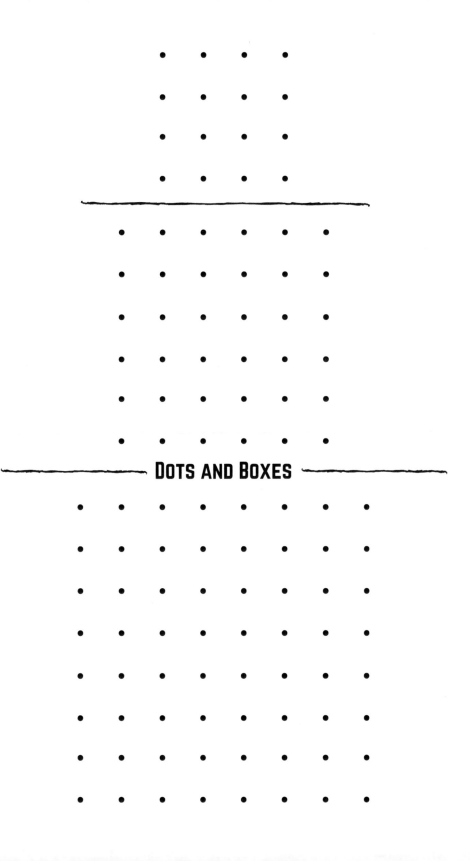

DOTS AND BOXES

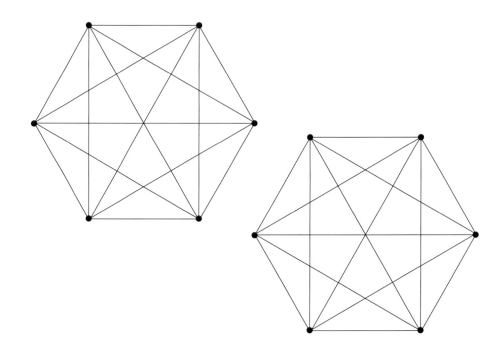

HEXAGON

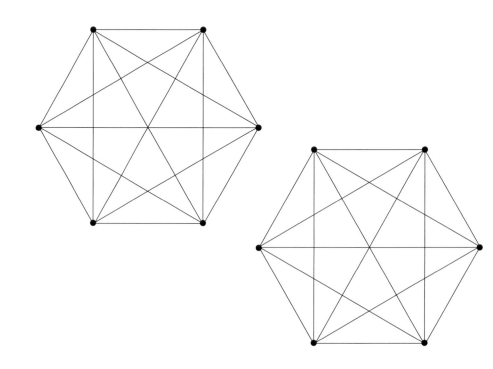

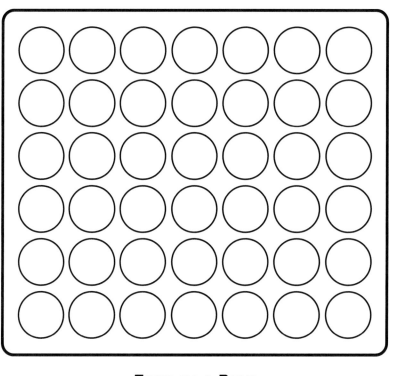

FOUR IN A ROW

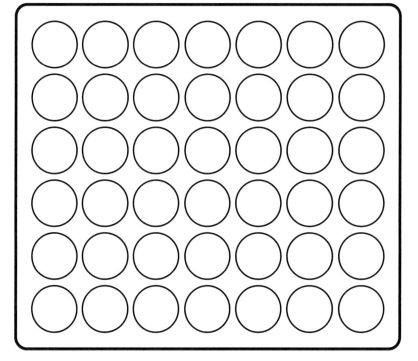

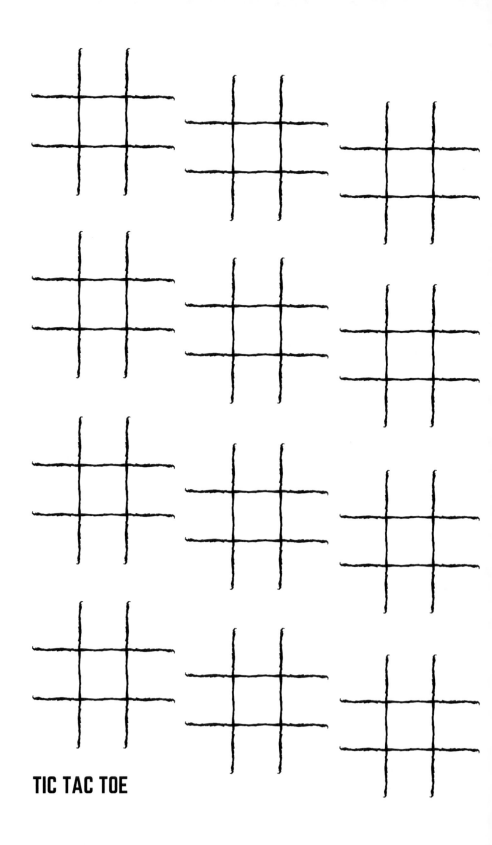

TIC TAC TOE

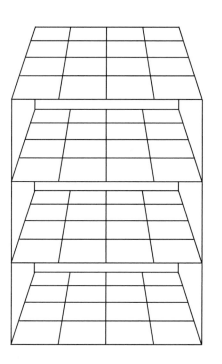

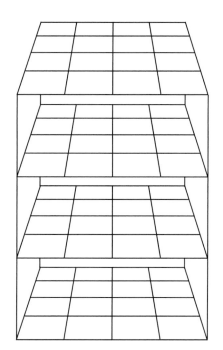

3D Tic Tac Toe

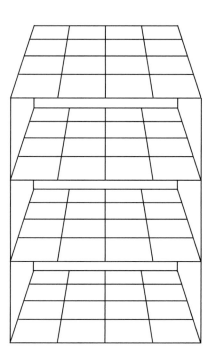

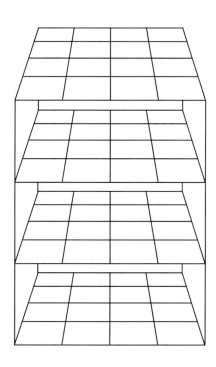

Obstruction

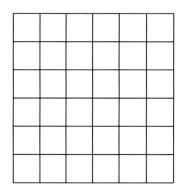

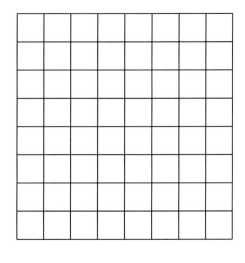

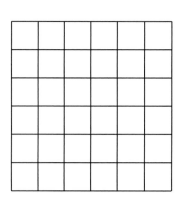

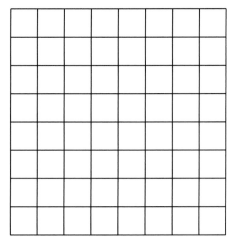

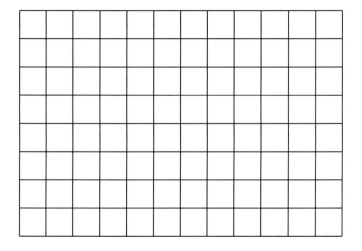

A	B	C	D	E
F	G	H	I	J
K	L	M	N	O
P	Q	R	S	T
U	V	W	X	Y
Z				

_ _ _ _ _ _ _ _ _ _

_ _ _ _ _ _ _ _ _ _

HANGMAN

A	B	C	D	E
F	G	H	I	J
K	L	M	N	O
P	Q	R	S	T
U	V	W	X	Y
Z				

_ _ _ _ _ _ _ _ _ _

_ _ _ _ _ _ _ _ _ _

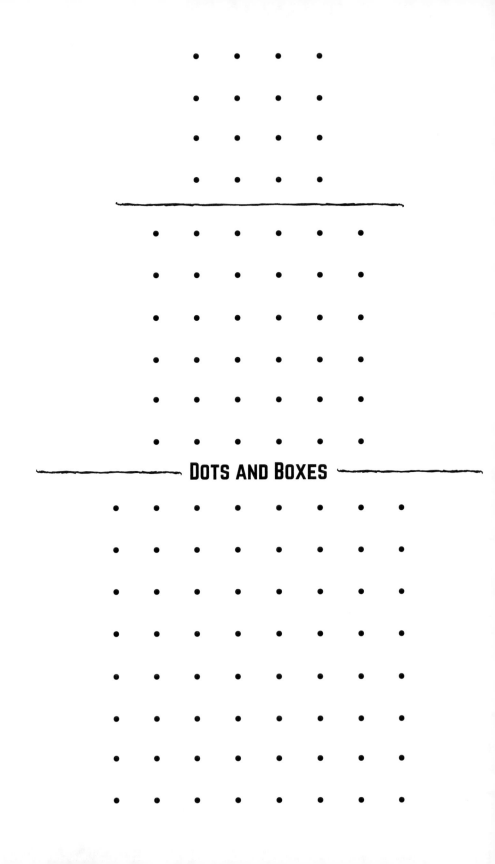

DOTS AND BOXES

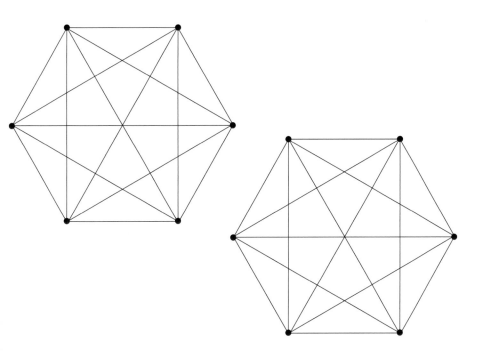

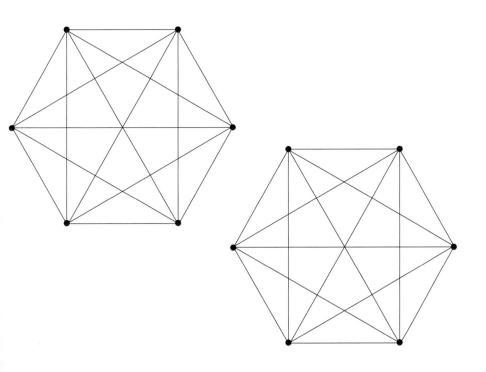

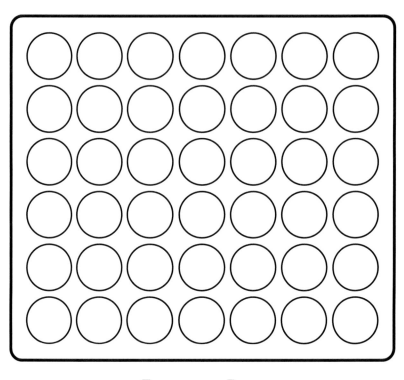

Four in a Row

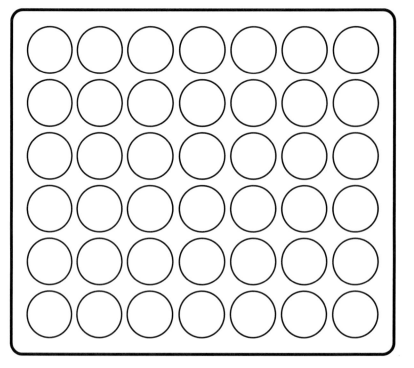

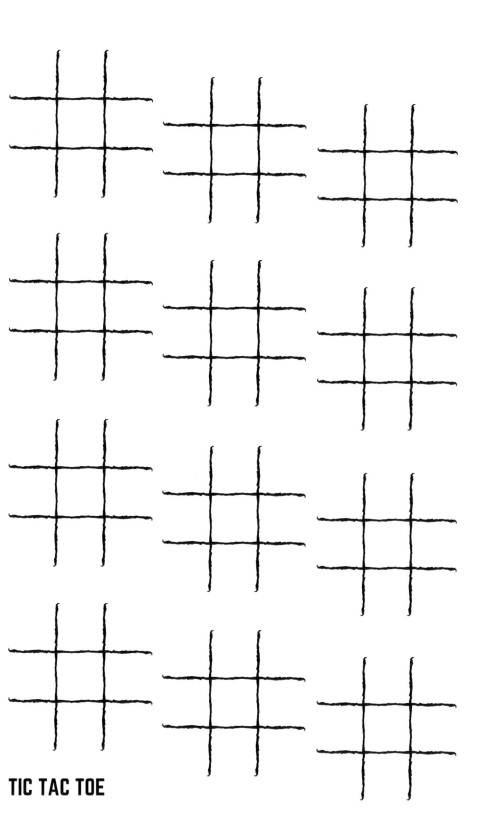

TIC TAC TOE

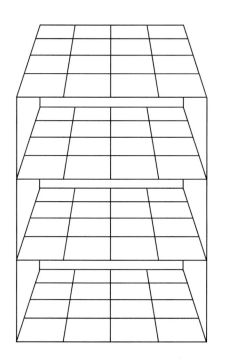

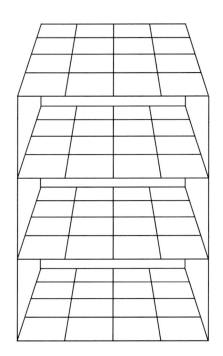

3D Tic Tac Toe

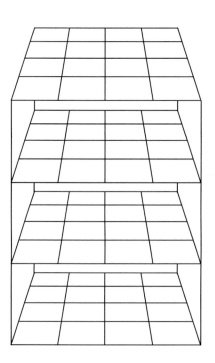

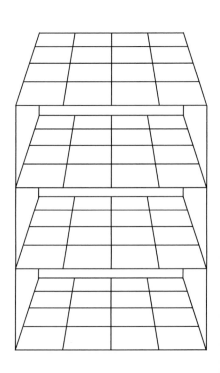

Obstruction

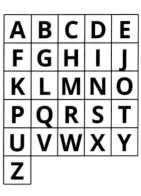

A	B	C	D	E
F	G	H	I	J
K	L	M	N	O
P	Q	R	S	T
U	V	W	X	Y
Z				

_ _ _ _ _ _ _ _ _

_ _ _ _ _ _ _ _ _

 **HANGMAN**

A	B	C	D	E
F	G	H	I	J
K	L	M	N	O
P	Q	R	S	T
U	V	W	X	Y
Z				

_ _ _ _ _ _ _ _ _

_ _ _ _ _ _ _ _ _

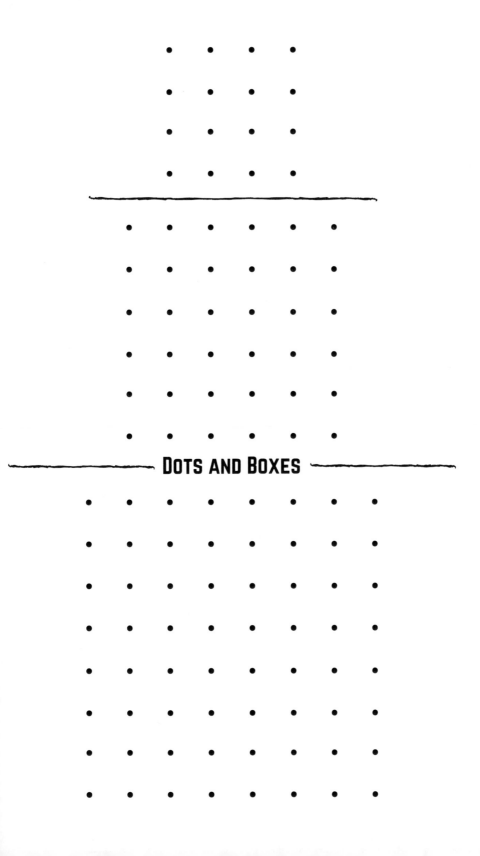

DOTS AND BOXES

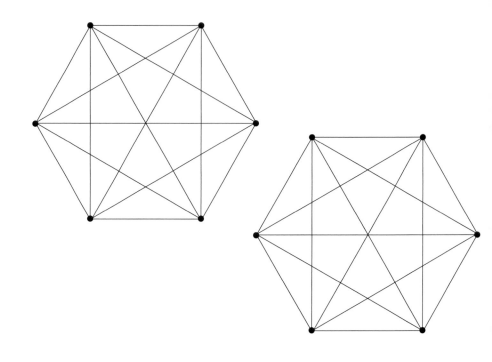

HEXAGON

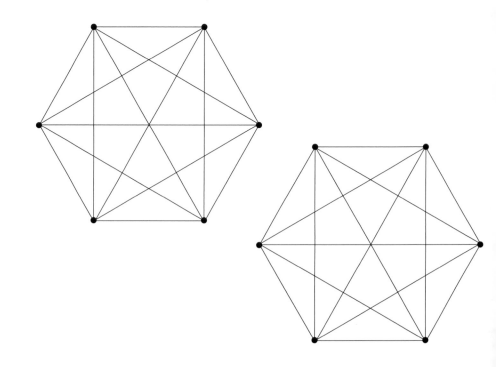

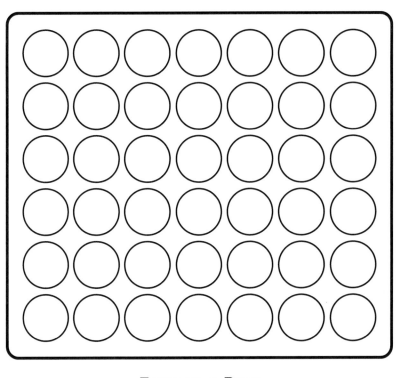

Four in a Row

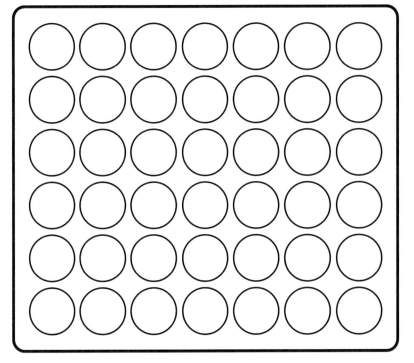

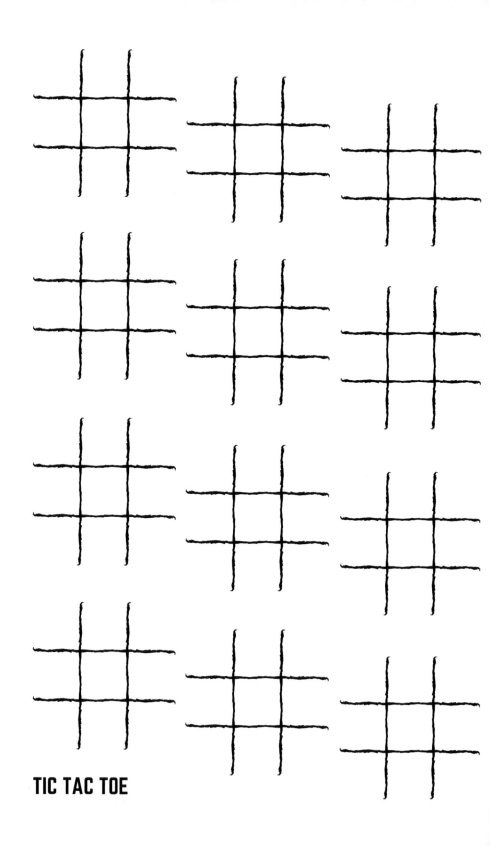

TIC TAC TOE

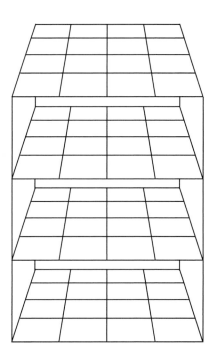

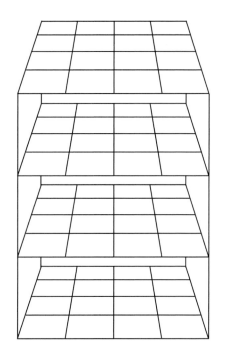

3D Tic Tac Toe

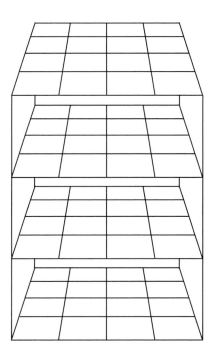

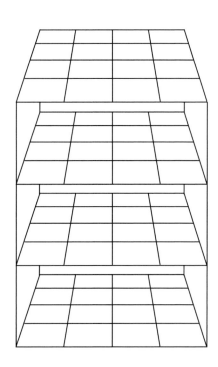

Obstruction

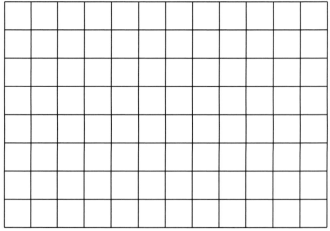

_ _ _ _ _ _ _ _ _ _ _ _ _

_ _ _ _ _ _ _ _ _ _ _ _

HANGMAN

_ _ _ _ _ _ _ _ _ _ _ _ _

_ _ _ _ _ _ _ _ _ _ _ _

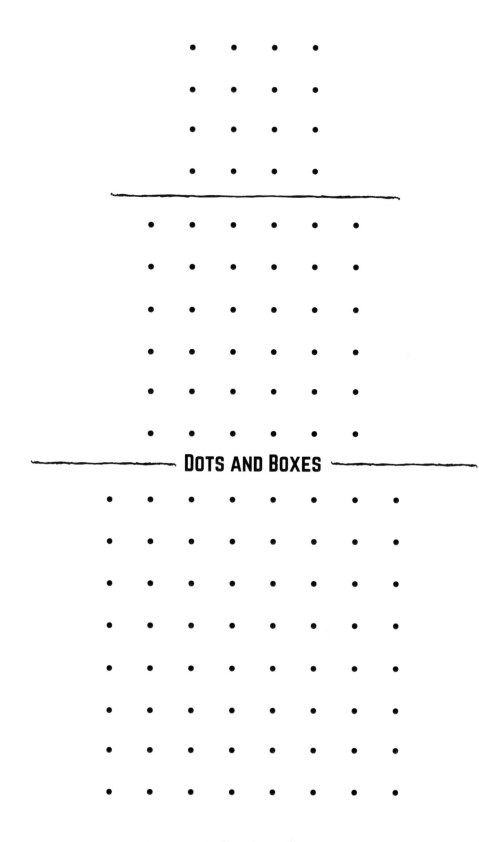

DOTS AND BOXES

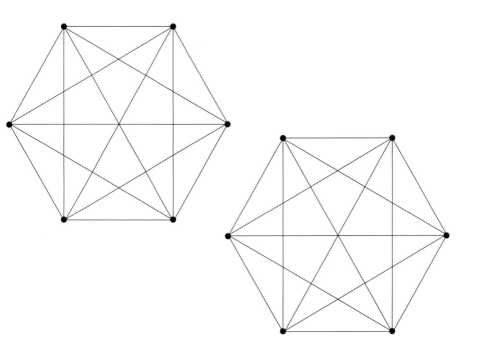

HEXAGON

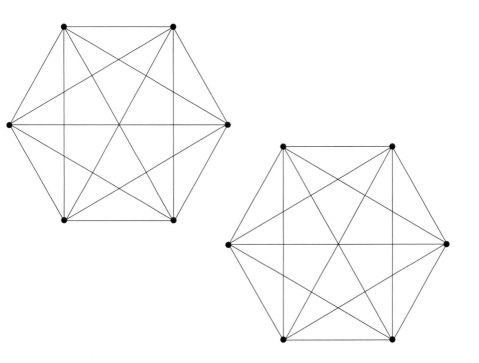

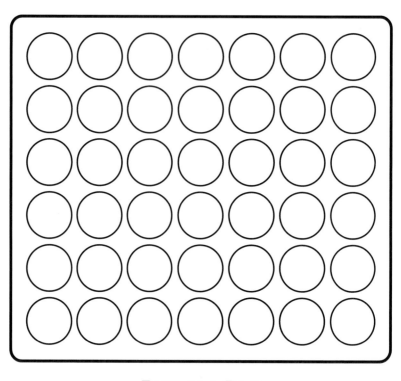

Four in a Row

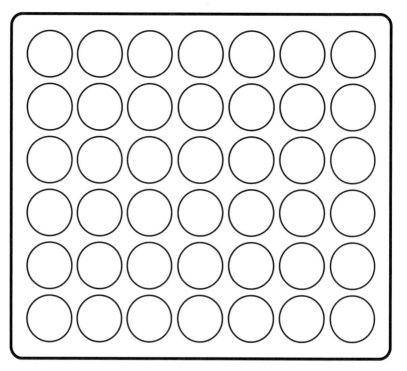

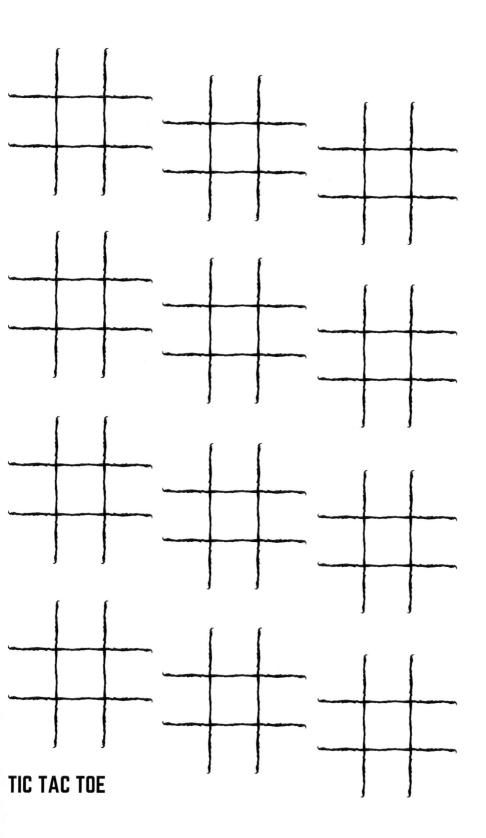

TIC TAC TOE

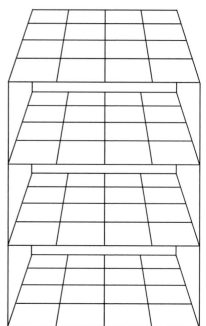
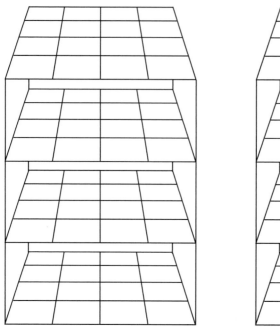

3D Tic Tac Toe

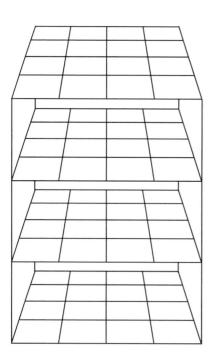
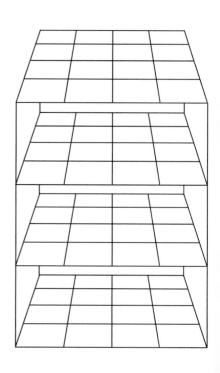

Obstruction

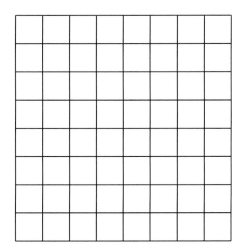

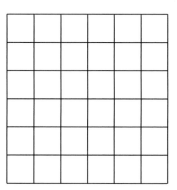

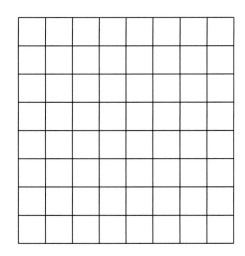

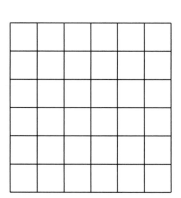

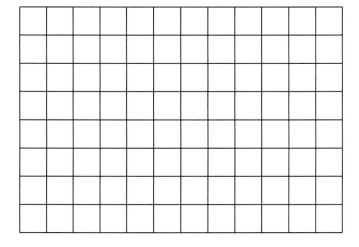

ABCDE
FGHIJ
KLMNO
PQRST
UVWXY
Z

_ _ _ _ _ _ _ _ _ _ _ _

_ _ _ _ _ _ _ _ _ _ _ _

HANGMAN

ABCDE
FGHIJ
KLMNO
PQRST
UVWXY
Z

_ _ _ _ _ _ _ _ _ _ _ _

_ _ _ _ _ _ _ _ _ _ _ _

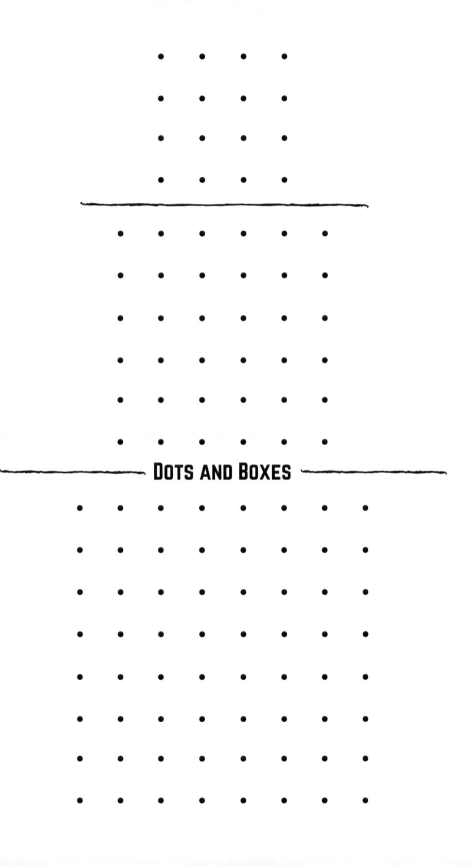

DOTS AND BOXES

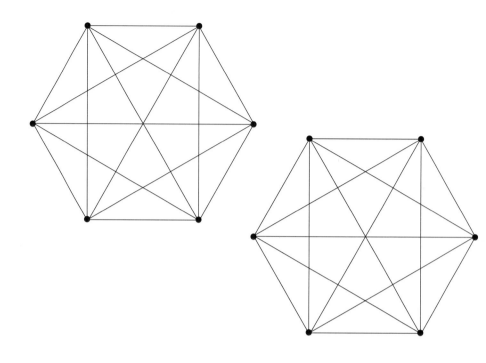

HEXAGON

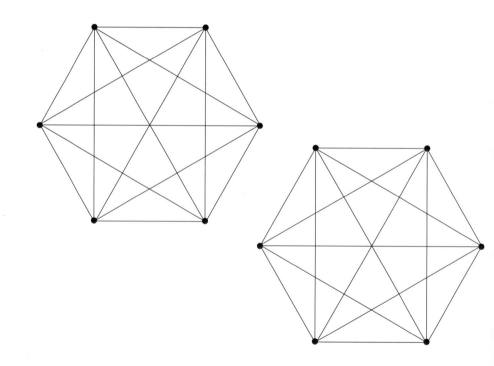

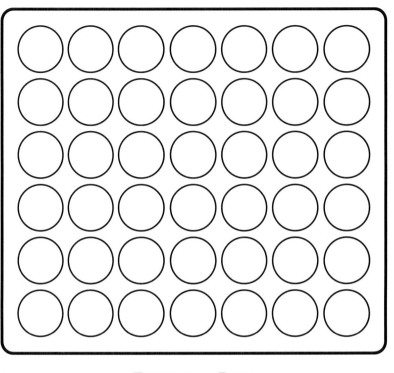

FOUR IN A ROW

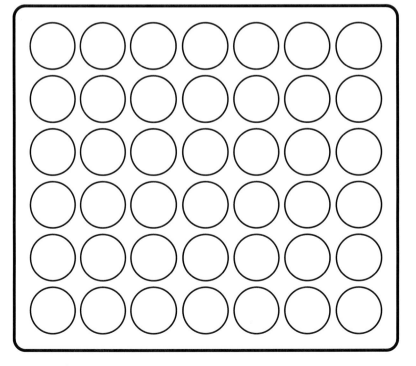

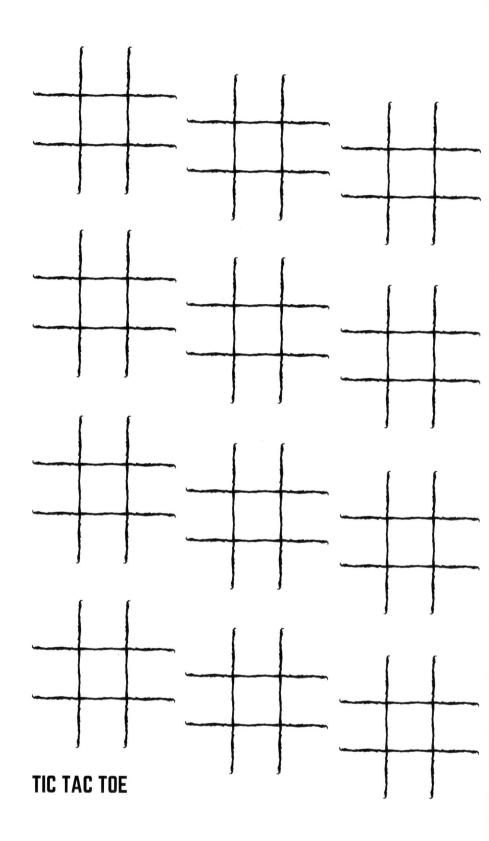

TIC TAC TOE

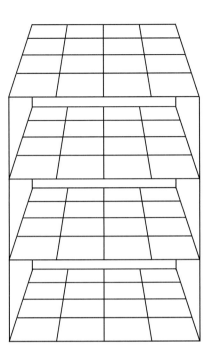

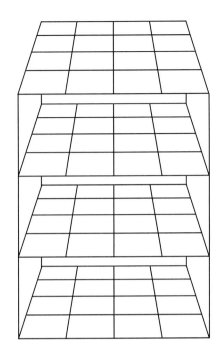

3D Tic Tac Toe

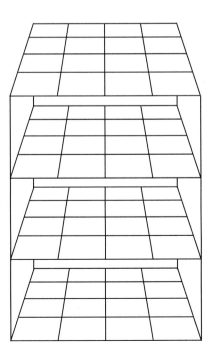

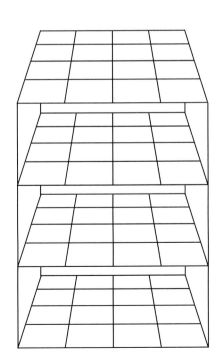

OBSTRUCTION

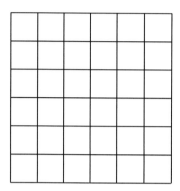

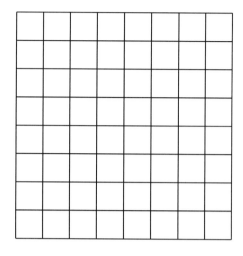

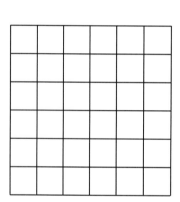

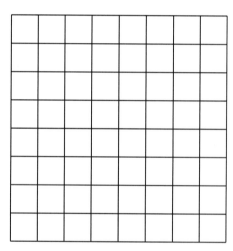

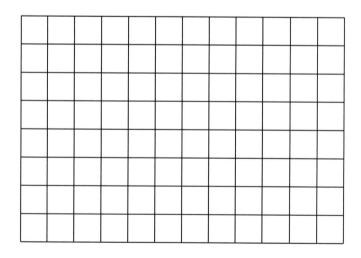

_ _ _ _ _ _ _ _ _ _ _

_ _ _ _ _ _ _ _ _ _ _

HANGMAN

_ _ _ _ _ _ _ _ _ _ _

_ _ _ _ _ _ _ _ _ _ _

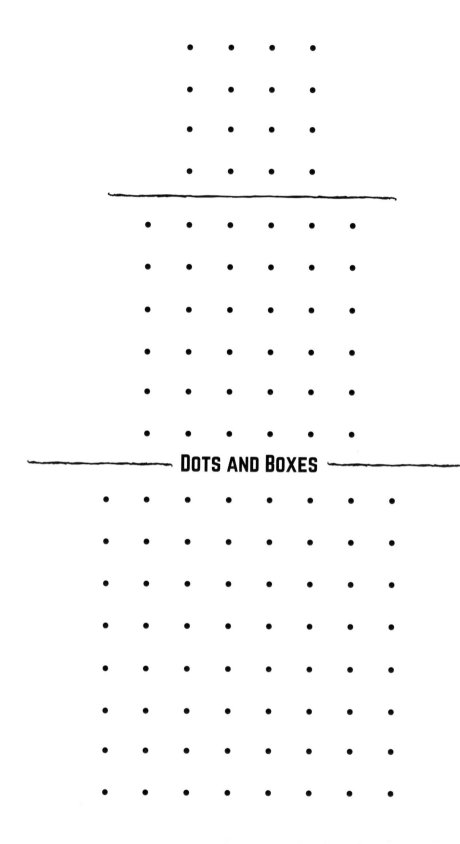

DOTS AND BOXES

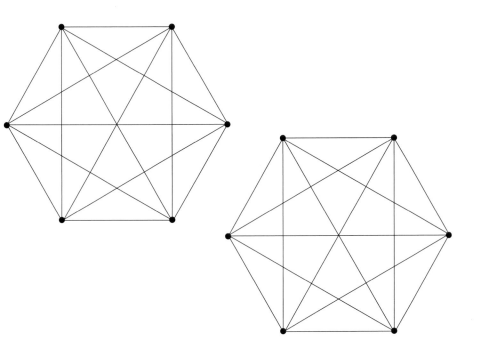

HEXAGON

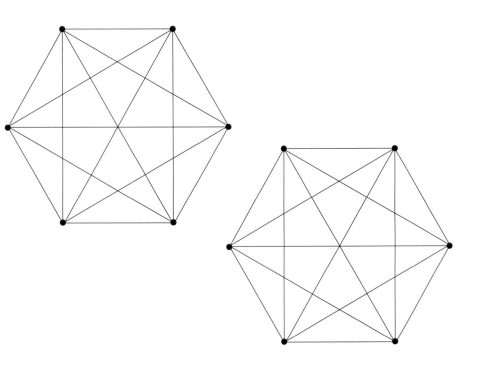

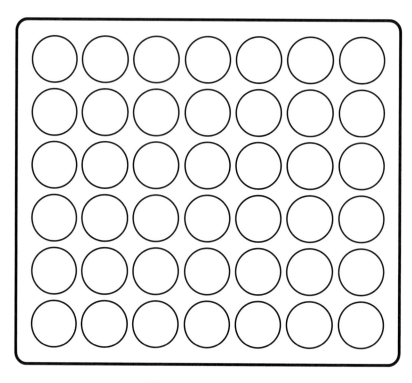

Four in a Row

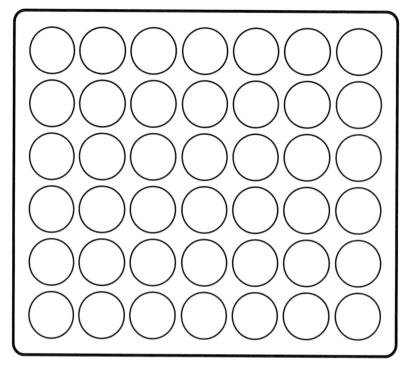

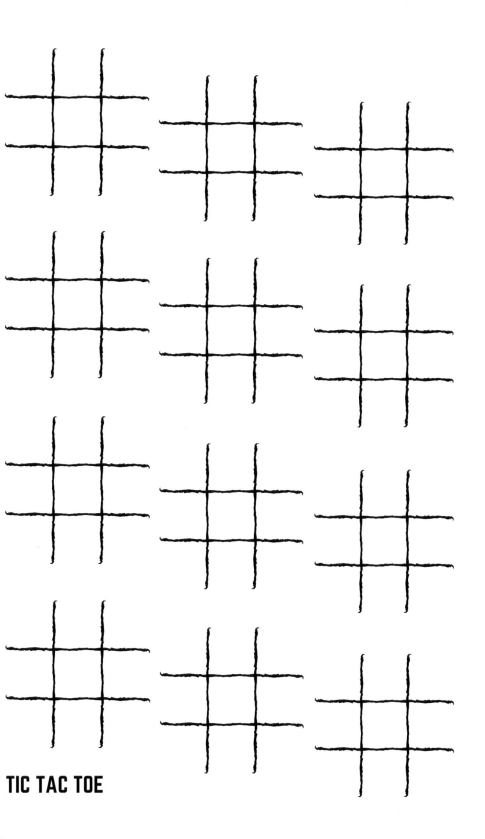

TIC TAC TOE

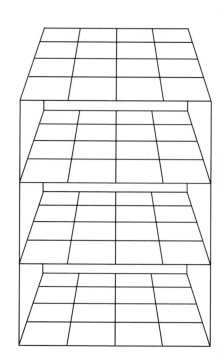

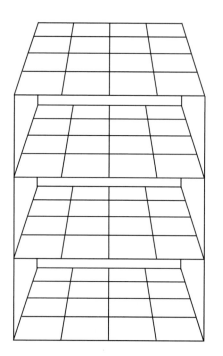

3D Tic Tac Toe

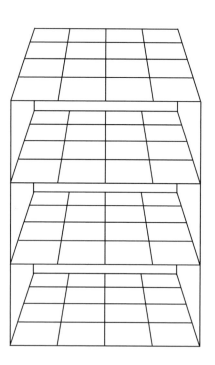

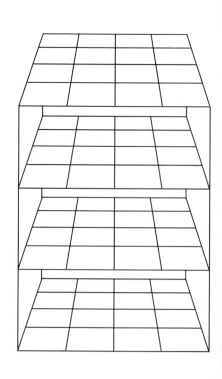

Obstruction

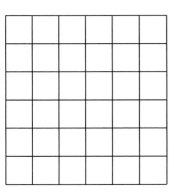

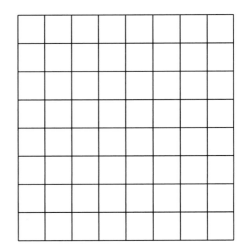

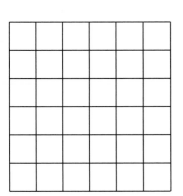

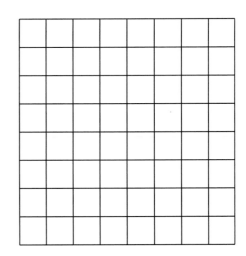

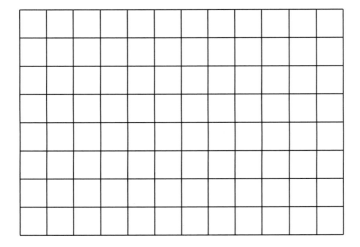

___ ___ ___ ___ ___ ___ ___ ___

___ ___ ___ ___ ___ ___ ___ ___

___ ___ ___ ___ ___ ___ ___ ___

___ ___ ___ ___ ___ ___ ___ ___

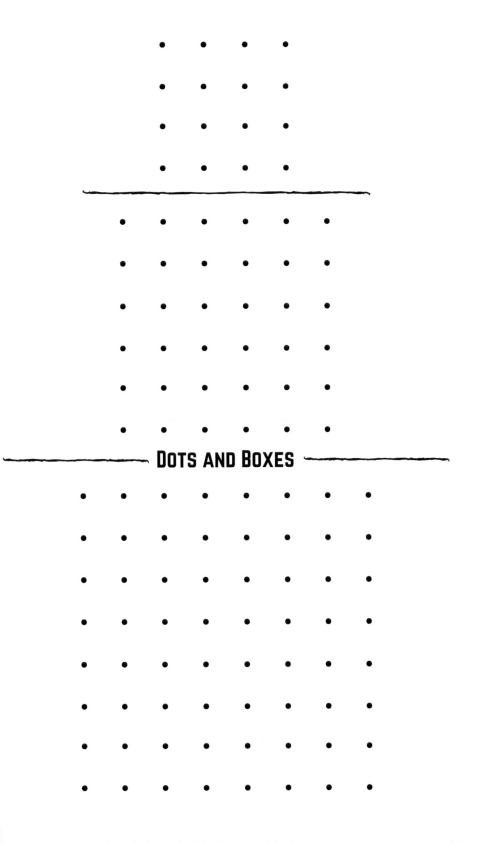

DOTS AND BOXES

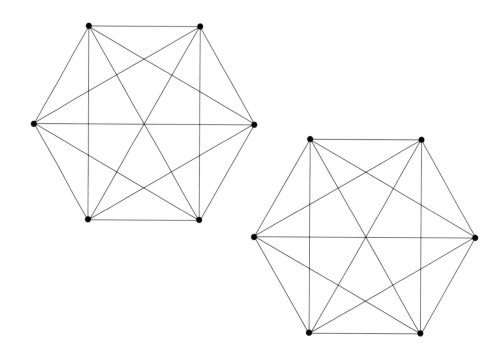

HEXAGON

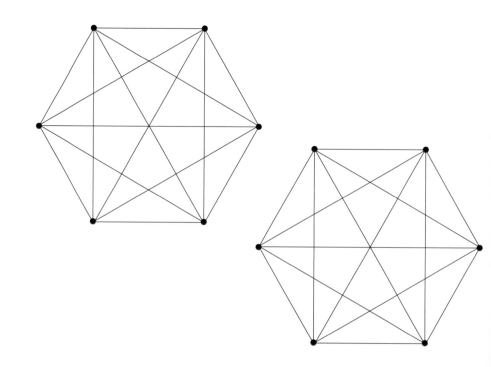

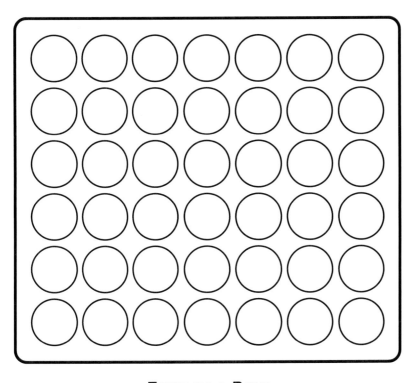

FOUR IN A ROW

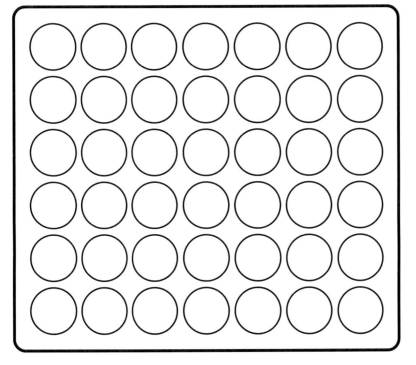

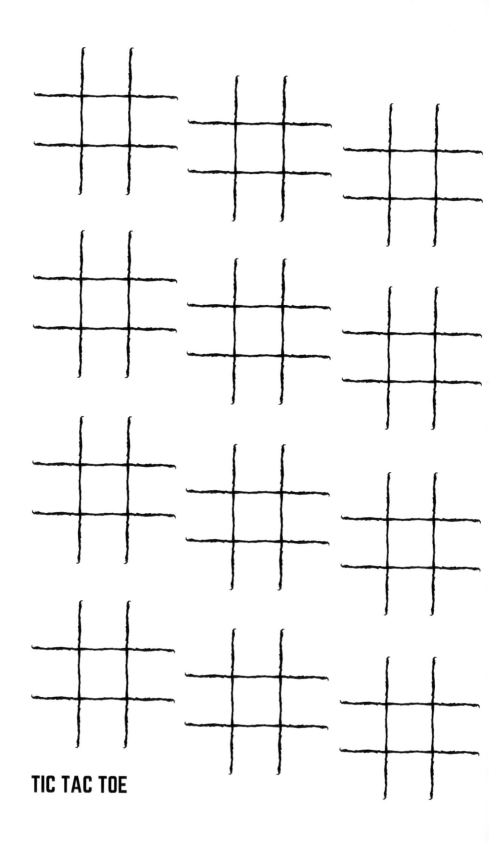

TIC TAC TOE

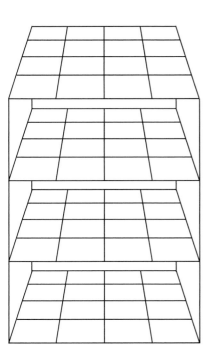
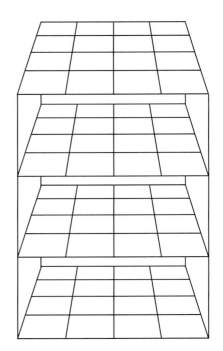

3D Tic Tac Toe

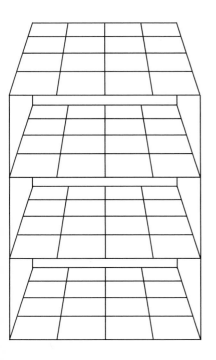
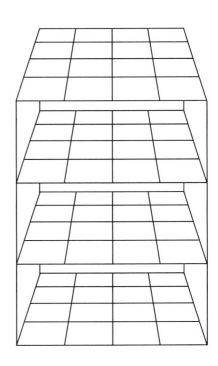

Obstruction

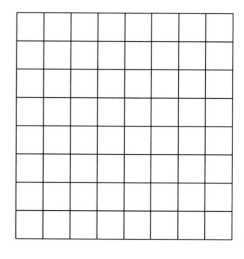

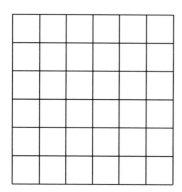

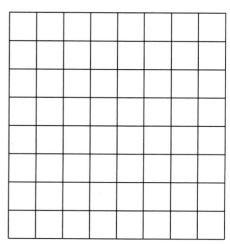

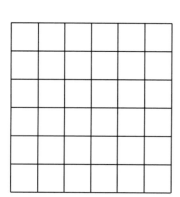

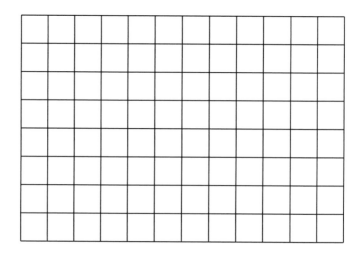

A	B	C	D	E
F	G	H	I	J
K	L	M	N	O
P	Q	R	S	T
U	V	W	X	Y
Z				

_ _ _ _ _ _ _ _ _ _

_ _ _ _ _ _ _ _ _ _

HANGMAN

A	B	C	D	E
F	G	H	I	J
K	L	M	N	O
P	Q	R	S	T
U	V	W	X	Y
Z				

_ _ _ _ _ _ _ _ _ _

_ _ _ _ _ _ _ _ _ _

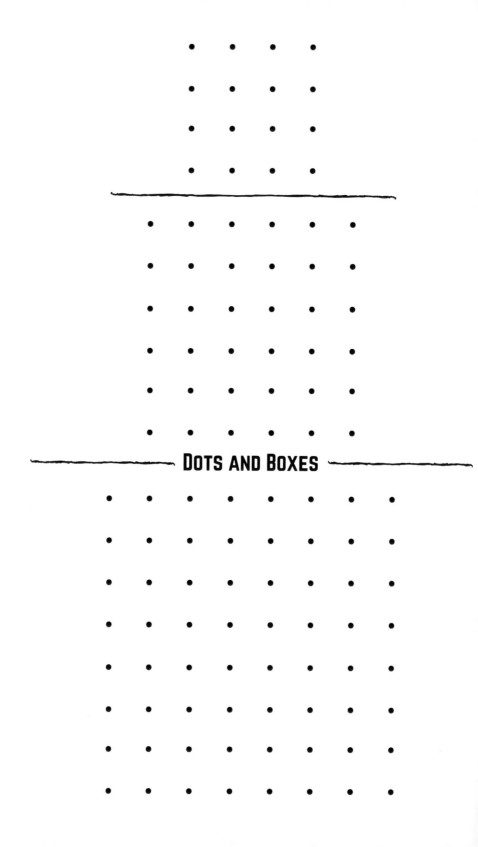

DOTS AND BOXES

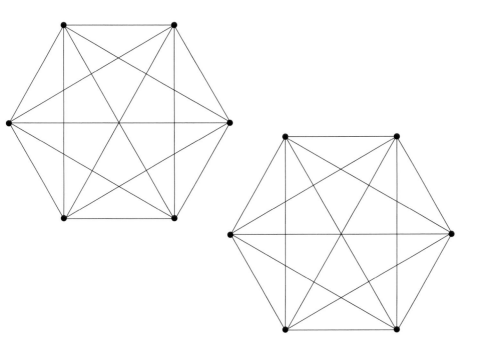

HEXAGON

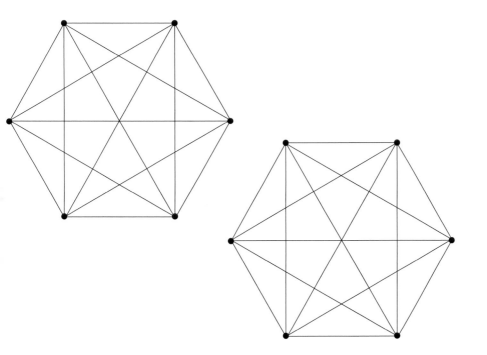

Four in a Row

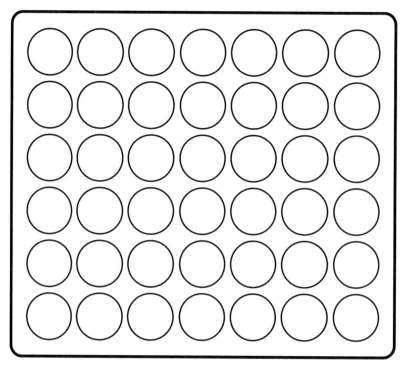

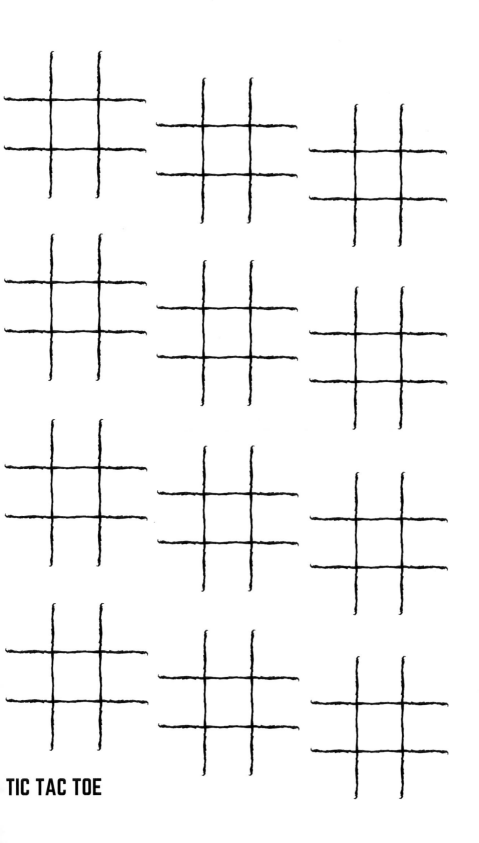

TIC TAC TOE

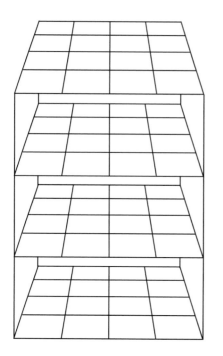
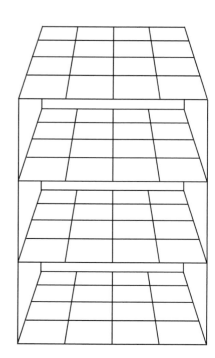

3D Tic Tac Toe

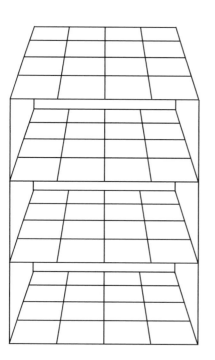
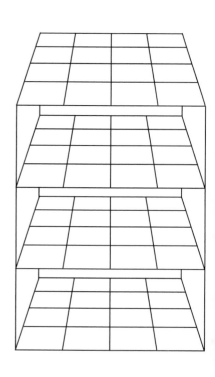

Obstruction

__ __ __ __ __ __ __ __ __ __

__ __ __ __ __ __ __ __ __ __

HANGMAN

__ __ __ __ __ __ __ __ __ __

__ __ __ __ __ __ __ __ __ __

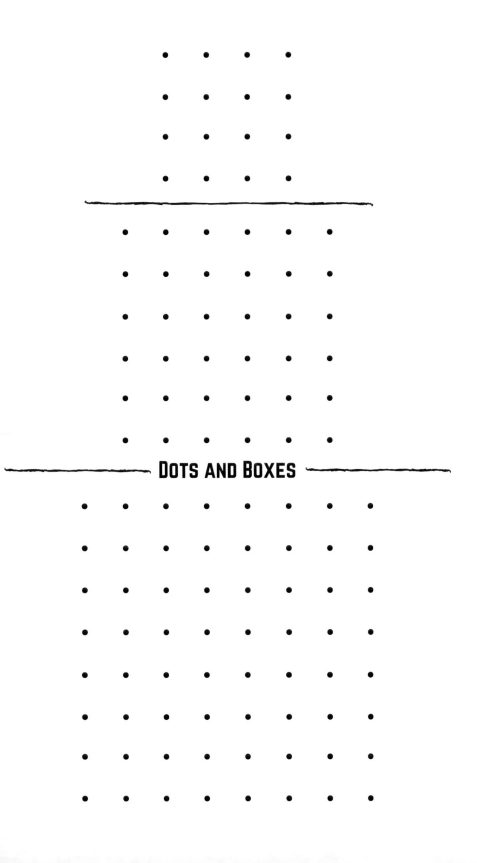

DOTS AND BOXES

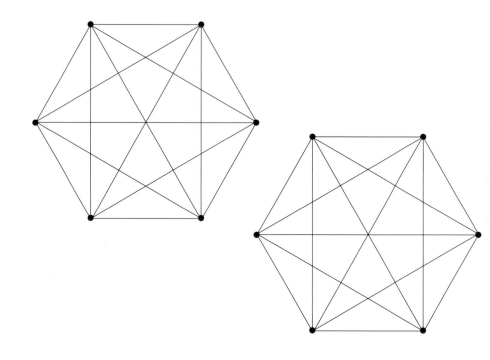

HEXAGON

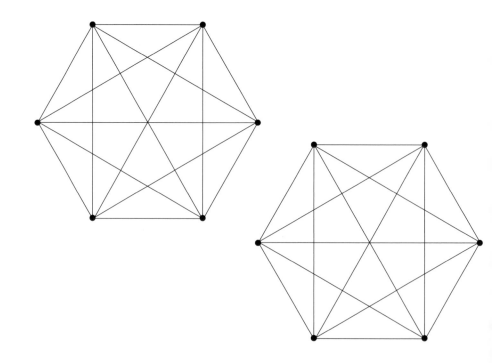

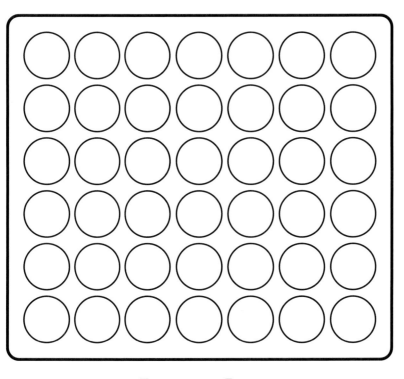

Four in a Row

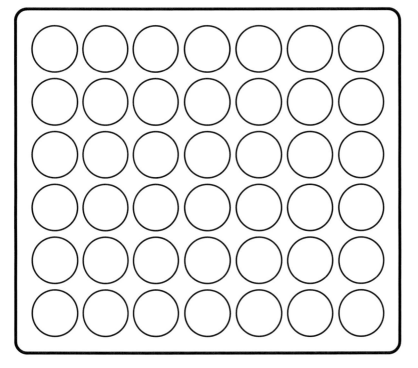

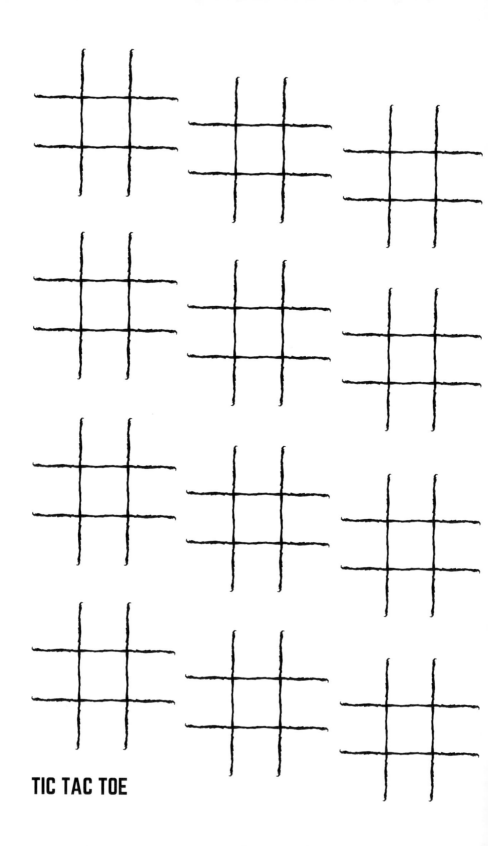

TIC TAC TOE

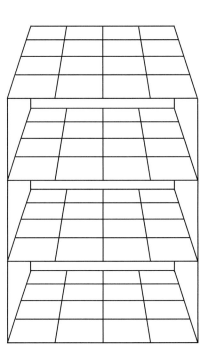

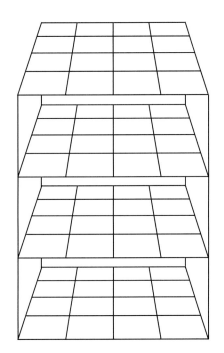

3D Tic Tac Toe

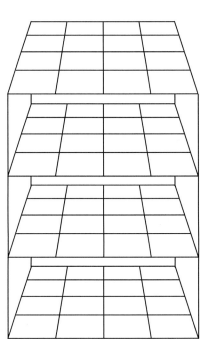

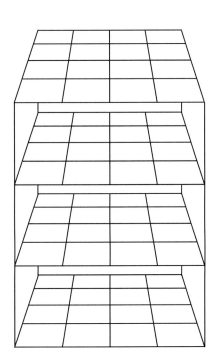

Obstruction

_ _ _ _ _ _ _ _ _ _

_ _ _ _ _ _ _ _ _ _

HANGMAN

_ _ _ _ _ _ _ _ _ _

_ _ _ _ _ _ _ _ _ _

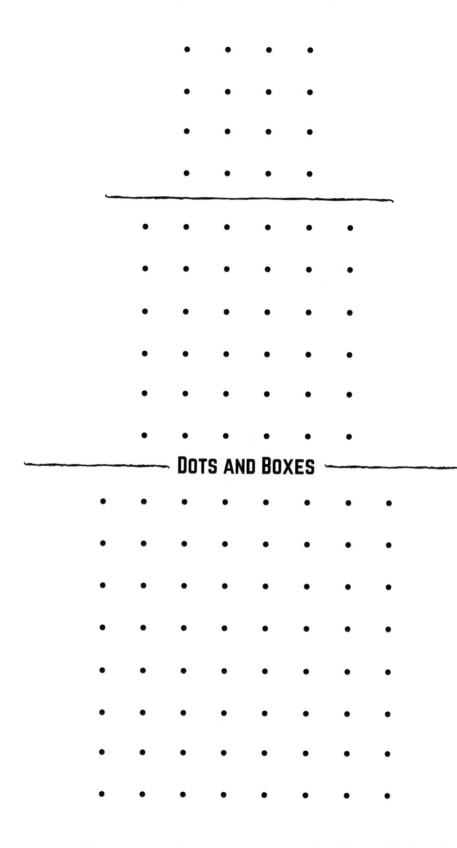

DOTS AND BOXES

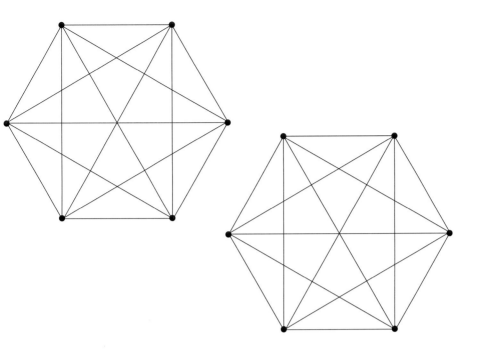

HEXAGON

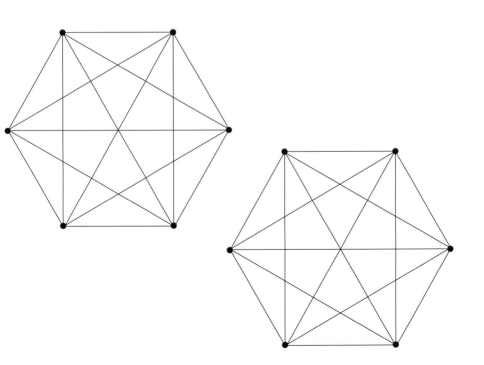

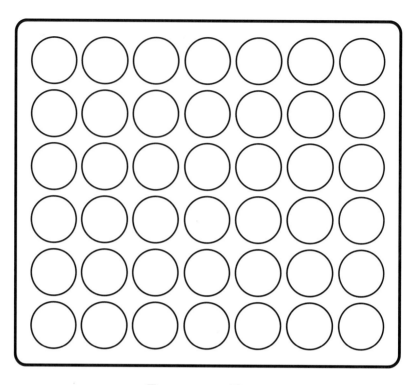

Four in a Row

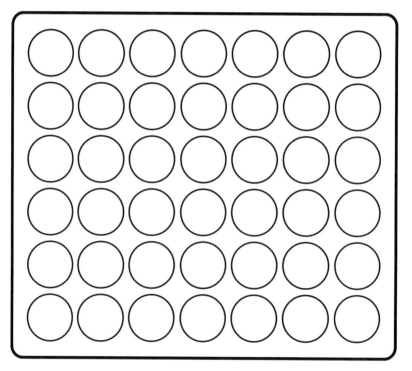

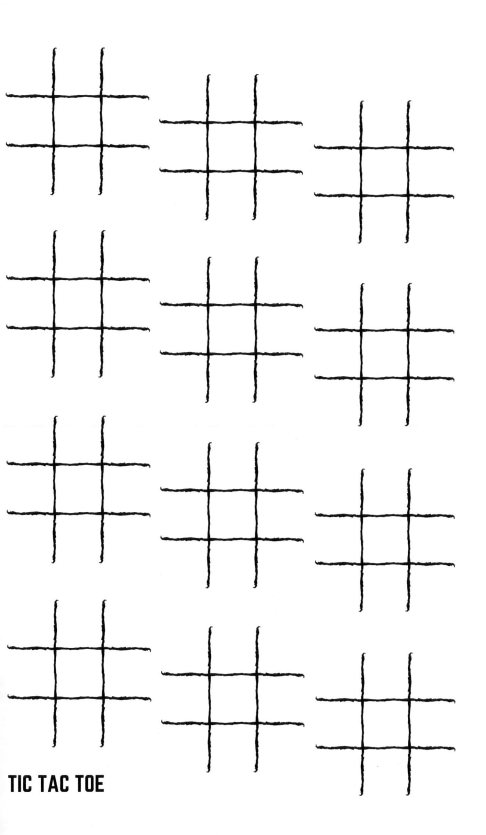

TIC TAC TOE

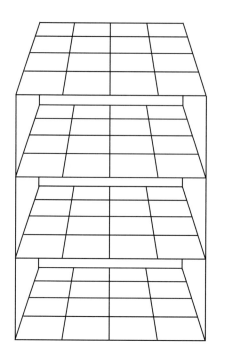 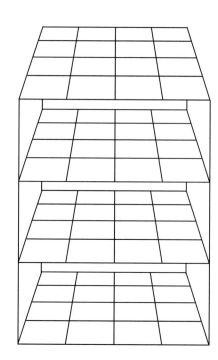

3D Tic Tac Toe

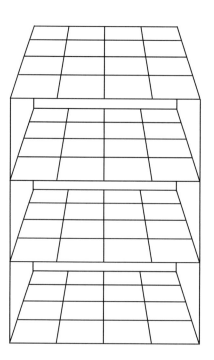 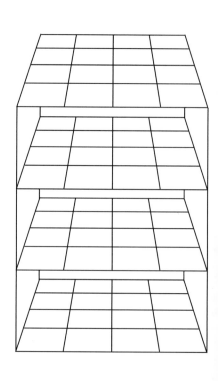

Obstruction

A B C D E
F G H I J
K L M N O
P Q R S T
U V W X Y
Z

＿ ＿ ＿ ＿ ＿ ＿ ＿ ＿ ＿ ＿

＿ ＿ ＿ ＿ ＿ ＿ ＿ ＿ ＿ ＿

HANGMAN

A B C D E
F G H I J
K L M N O
P Q R S T
U V W X Y
Z

＿ ＿ ＿ ＿ ＿ ＿ ＿ ＿ ＿ ＿

＿ ＿ ＿ ＿ ＿ ＿ ＿ ＿ ＿ ＿

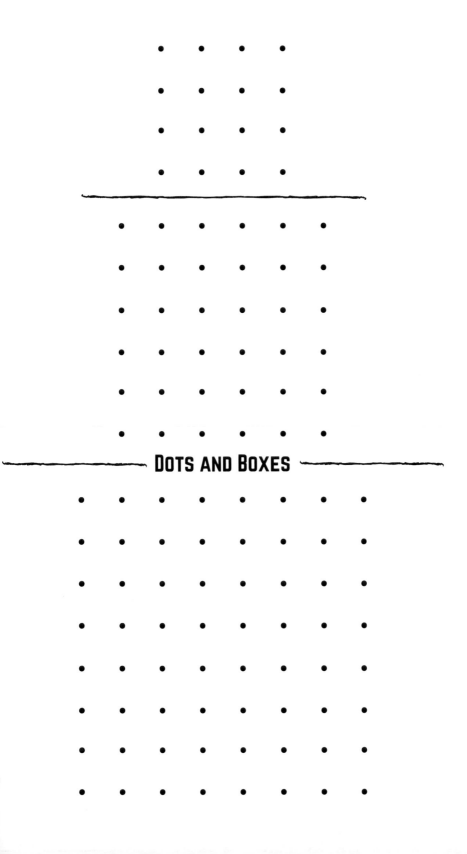

DOTS AND BOXES

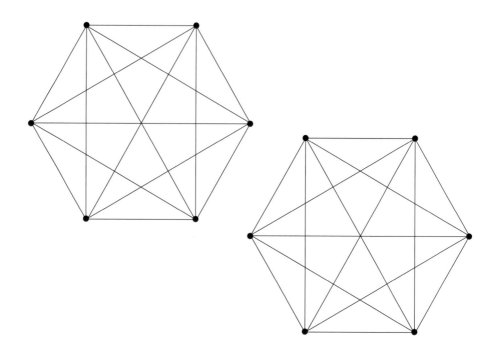

HEXAGON

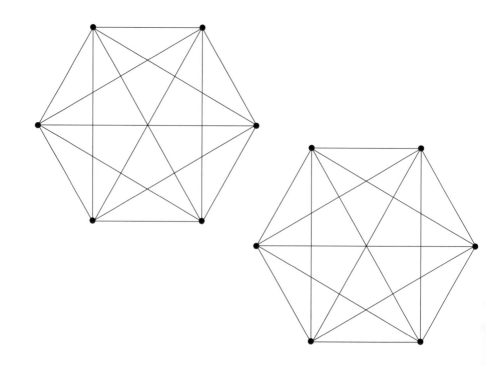

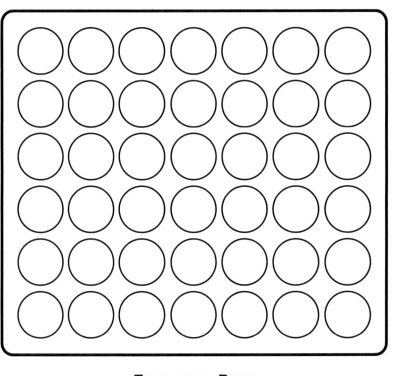

Four in a Row

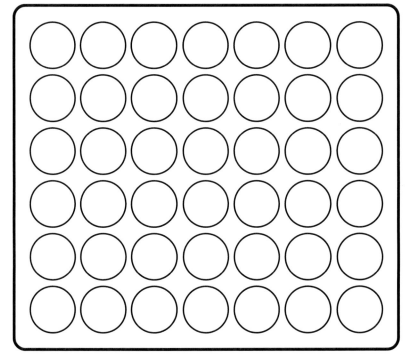

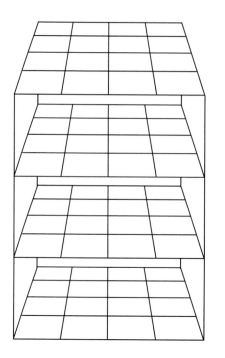

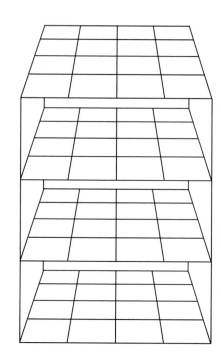

3D Tic Tac Toe

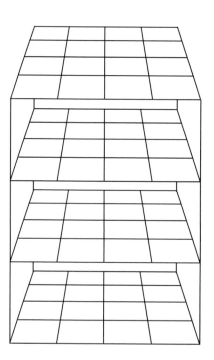

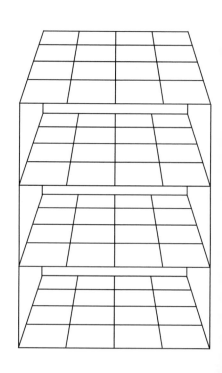

A B C D E
F G H I J
K L M N O
P Q R S T
U V W X Y
Z

_ _ _ _ _ _ _ _ _ _ _

_ _ _ _ _ _ _ _ _ _ _

HANGMAN

A B C D E
F G H I J
K L M N O
P Q R S T
U V W X Y
Z

_ _ _ _ _ _ _ _ _ _ _

_ _ _ _ _ _ _ _ _ _ _

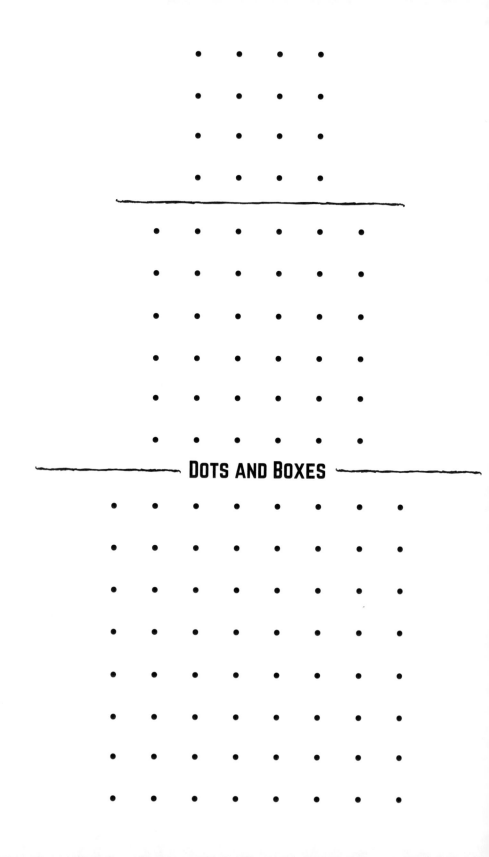

DOTS AND BOXES

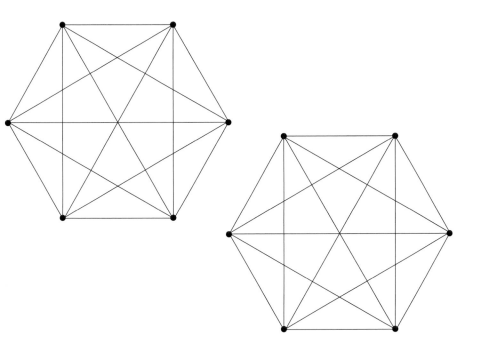

HEXAGON

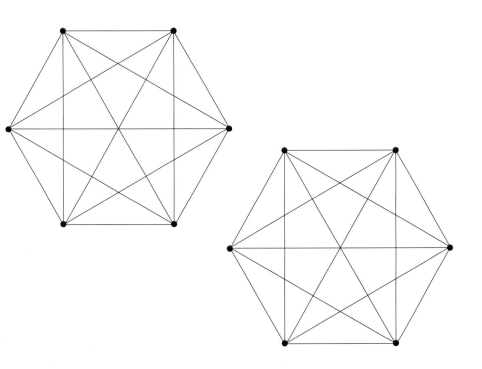

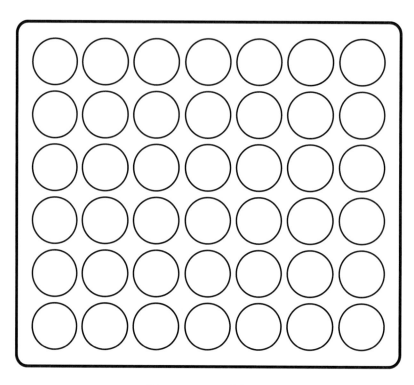

FOUR IN A ROW

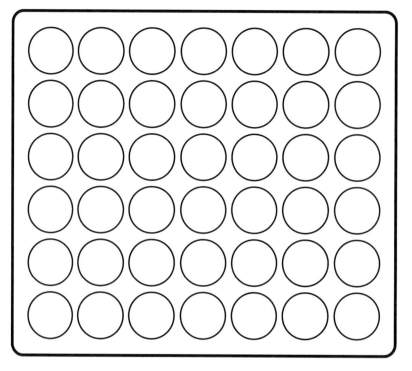

Made in United States
North Haven, CT
11 July 2022

21210059R00067